T0247623

LANDSCAPE AS WEAPON

LANDSCAPE
AS WEAPON
CULTURES OF EXHAUSTION
AND REFUSAL

JOHN BECK

REAKTION BOOKS

To Monk and Fisher

Published by Reaktion Books Ltd
Unit 32, Waterside
44–48 Wharf Road
London N1 7UX, UK
www.reaktionbooks.co.uk

First published 2021
Copyright © John Beck 2021

Printed and bound in Great Britain
by TJ Books Limited, Padstow, Cornwall

A catalogue record for this book is available from the British Library

ISBN 978 1 78914 305 8

CONTENTS

Introduction

In March 2019 a major new exhibition by British artist Mike Nelson opened in Tate Britain's Duveen Galleries. Titled *The Asset Strippers*, Nelson assembled in the grand sculpture court a stockpile of industrial and agricultural machinery, timber and metal gleaned from online auctions of company liquidations. Knitting machines, weighing scales, cement mixers, filing cabinets, drill bits, milling machines and tarpaulins were laid out, sometimes stacked, with the space partitioned using wood salvaged from a Victorian Ministry of Defence barracks and NHS hospital doors. The exhibition displayed with incongruous care the remains of what was once the apparatus of British productivity.

The days when the exhibition of non-art stuff in elite galleries might be considered challenging are long over, and part of the point of a show like *The Asset Strippers* is for visitors to recognize the art historical references, from Duchamp and Picabia through to Rauschenberg, Paolozzi, Caro, Serra and so on. Reviews of the exhibition took pleasure in detecting echoes of iconic artworks in the machines. In *The Observer*, for instance, Laura Cumming claimed that a 'compressed chunk of metal, perhaps some kind of boiler, steel-grey and truculent, exactly resembles Max Ernst's *Celebes*'.[1] It is hard not to see art in an art gallery. The history of twentieth-century art gives permission for this sort of curatorial indexing and is integral to the capacity of *The Asset Strippers* to generate associations among, and pose questions about, art, industry and commerce. Nelson is comfortable pulling into view the notion of the gallery as a warehouse full of saleable objects, but the light touch does not diminish the seriousness of the questions the exhibition raises about economic decline, redundancy and opportunistic exploitation. One of the key insights established by the Duchampian ready-made in relation to art – that value is dependent on context – is here recycled on a grand scale, along with the objects themselves that are converted, through the magic of rescue by the artist, from bankrupt stock to cultural capital. Like Baudelaire's ragpicker, that long-standing model for modernist labour, Nelson embraces that which others have discarded. 'All that the city has rejected,' Baudelaire wrote in 1851, 'all it has lost, shunned, disdained, broken, this man catalogs and stores. He sifts through the archives of debauch, the junkyards of scrap. He creates order, makes an intelligent choice; like a miser hoarding treasure, he gathers the refuse that has been spit out by the god of Industry, to make of it objects of delight or utility.'[2]

Objects of delight or utility. Beyond the art historically familiar, in *The Asset Strippers* Nelson taps into what is, by now, a generations-long embrace of saving apparently useless old stuff. Second-hand, retro, vintage, recycled, upcycled, preloved: the vocabulary used to describe the passionate preservation of remnants of the past has flourished along with the mainstream embrace of what used to be the preserve of a self-consciously recondite and culturally marginal sensibility. We live in the age of the patina. The wipe-clean surfaces of modernity hold no allure and no mysteries; instead, real value is to be found in the unbleached, grease-stained, sweat-burnished remains of the workshops and factories that built that world. The objects made in those factories have taken their place in antique shops, auction sites and flea markets, which is to be expected. What is perhaps novel about the current relation to the recent past is that it is not just the furniture, couture and nostalgic gewgaws of childhood that remain auratic objects of desire, but the machines and tools that turned them out and the overalls worn by the workers on the assembly lines, boiler rooms, ridges and furrows of past times.

What, in the end, is most confusing about *The Asset Strippers* is that, despite its overly signposted art historical and sociopolitical references, I still liked it. I liked it even though I disapproved of nearly everything about it. There appears to be something irresistibly attractive about old machinery even to the non-mechanically inclined. The colours, the branding, the complexity of the construction and the ingenuity of the design; the painterly surfaces produced by years of use and misuse; the much-heralded patina beloved by the vintage hound; the alien presence of a very heavy object that did – and might still do – something. *The Asset Strippers* is, at once, almost unbearably poignant and insufferably precious. The branded goods and trade names call forth a world of local entrepreneurship that, for a twenty-first-century audience, is probably more familiar to viewers of *Wallace and Gromit* than professionals in contemporary manufacturing. The stacking of the objects contributes in no small part to the invitation to wonder: it is not so much the way the makeshift plinths elevate the stuff in an ironic gesture towards their sculptural status in the gallery, but the fact that it is reminiscent of the kind of Spielberg magic capable of transforming the everyday by just shuffling the pieces. Were these immovable objects piled up by some poltergeist or extraterrestrial? They seem to have been effortlessly deposited or discovered, like the Second World War planes in *Close Encounters of the Third Kind* that mysteriously reappear in the desert after thirty years.[3]

This is all part of the charm of *The Asset Strippers*, the way it flirts with sci-fi, collecting and hipster retail (in the promotional photos Nelson could be modelling for a Japanese menswear designer, all distressed vintage denim, knitted hat and salt-and-pepper facial foliage). It is a work of seduction; it invites visitors to luxuriate in the presence of what we have learned to see as beautiful old things without complications. This is the post-industrial world, where everything that has been preloved or unloved or forgotten can be reloved, revived, repositioned as art, as a collectible, a piece. It is a world where factories and factory labour have been sent far away, out of sight and beyond the experience of consumers, so that big, dirty machines are so marvellous to behold that they must have come from another age or from Mars.

Where, though, are the asset strippers of the title? The artist has rescued the assets that have been stripped, but the sellers, not to mention the people for whom the assets were tools, remain absent. There is so much missing in *The Asset Strippers*. It is the absence of context that makes the retrieved remnants so compelling as things, as forms, and that also makes visible the decontextualizing violence of art galleries and museums. The missing factories, missing workers, missing products, missing bosses, as well as the missing noise and movement – it is the missing economic and social history that might account for the invention, use and redundancy of all the objects gathered in the exhibition that Nelson manages, negatively, to invoke. In its summoning of the departed, absconded or unreachable, Nelson's exhibition taps into a common aspect of much recent cultural work: a preoccupation with ghosts.

The Asset Strippers speaks to the concerns of this book in a number of ways. It addresses a set of cultural preoccupations that have become familiar – an obsession with the past that ranges from a profound sense of loss to an aestheticizing of the material remains of old things, big and small; a fascination with what is taken as the authenticity of old things, especially those related to labour and with production in particular; a sense that we are living amid the ruins or among the relics of a lost world; a foreshortened sense of the future and a fascination with so-called retro-futures, old versions of the future now positioned as missed opportunities; a sense of concealed, absent or inaccessible spaces and things.

The topics addressed here circle around a number of these issues, especially as they pertain to matters of space and time – of temporality in its spatial extensions across the country and the city, and in its contested and reworked forms as public symbols or markers. A good deal of what follows is concerned with the stuff that is left behind – the abandoned or discarded, used up, exhausted: the remains. And a fair amount of the cultural work discussed here is concerned with working among, and with, the remains – the scraps, the edges, the wasted. Decommissioned military sites, post-industrial spaces, depopulated countryside, contested or forgotten zones between sites, monuments to forgotten heroes. Places where things once happened, never happened, might yet happen.

It is no surprise that writers, artists and film-makers have for so long been drawn to unproductive and abandoned spaces, not only because they are cheap and available but because they can be imagined as 'raw' material, as the unmediated, last remaining vestiges of the wild – the thing itself. As such, wasteland in its various forms can serve as the embodiment of a long-standing bohemian identification with the aberrant – with the abject, corrupt, unrepentant, slothful, contemptuous residuum of bourgeois society. The wasted or abandoned space, its value already extracted by a predatory world, is nothing but critical potentiality – it is the ultimate modern space of refusal, an authentic ground zero, an actually existing material out of which new worlds might be made.

The problem with this vision of refusenik creativity on the margins – if it is indeed a problem – is that it has been thoroughly absorbed into the culture to the point where it, too, is an exhausted shadow of its former emaciated glory. As we will see, it is not only the grand achievements of the past that have enjoyed a retrofit, but the garbage of the old days – the rural poverty, the housing estates and high rises, the secret military bases, the footholds of empire, the industrial sludge and subterranean effluent of advanced industrial societies. Once forgotten or ignored, and only dragged into the light by radicals and the avant-garde, the rubbish of history is now everywhere, reclaimed and memorialized, celebrated and circulated. There are special sections in bookshops and programmes on television.

Even this argument about the commodification of dissent is old news, and it is not my aim to simply revisit that story here. What does seem important, nevertheless, is the continual and sustained focus, in a wide range of books, films, visual art and other cultural work, on the prospects for a landscape capable of supporting, framing or embodying modes of life critical of, or counter to, contemporary forms of capitalist exploitation and oppression. The focus here, then, is not on the sell out as such but on the struggle. The struggle is not merely between critical practices and official narratives, but often takes the form of a complex dance – at once seductive and hostile – between a dissident vision and a ferocious culture of ravenous consumption. This is why, for me, *The*

LANDSCAPE AS WEAPON

Asset Strippers seems to capture something significant about early twenty-first-century late capitalist culture: it is simultaneously trite and profound, seductive and horrific. It is about exhaustion and loss, but also, possibly, about subversion and refusal.

My concern with landscape in this book is not solely about representations of places but it does insist upon the role of landscape as a representational practice. In other words, landscape here is not just a synonym for space or territory, but is about how places are figured, made, built and taken apart, how they are made to look and signify, what they say through the shapes they are made to adopt. It is also about how places push back, how they interfere, prompt and demand modes of attention and intervention. Landscape, in short, is about the entangled shaping of space, perception and representation.

When uncontested, landscape serves a largely normative function. As a physical form the landscape, to the extent that it is taken as the site upon which life is grounded, works as a means, as geographer Don Mitchell argues, of naturalizing social relations and making them seem inevitable. Landscape, then, can often be seen as an achieved fact, as just the way things are, rather than as a constructed thing. Don Mitchell suggests that in order to be transformed, landscape 'has to be taken apart, thrown into disarray, literally disintegrated as a landscape'.[4] W.J.T. Mitchell has similarly written that he wanted to change landscape from a noun to a verb so that landscape might be thought, not just 'as an object to be seen or a text to be read, but as a process by which social and subjective identities are formed'. Thinking of landscape in this way would mean not only asking what landscape is or means, but 'what it *does*, how it works as a cultural practice'.[5]

As a motivated way of seeing, landscape is a mode of scene-making capable not only of challenging the naturalized order of the status quo and revealing it as such, but of modelling alternative realities, reshaped and retooled stages of, and for, action. The extent to which we are prepared to consider the maintenance of the status quo as a form of naturalized domination might stand as a measure of how far we are prepared to entertain the prospect of landscape (both physical and representational) as already a tool for shaping reality. The kind of defamiliarization Nelson achieves in *The Asset Strippers* is made possible through the relocation of objects, but the decontextualization of these metonyms for labour, while raising questions about industry, finance and work, also runs the risk of encouraging attention solely to formal issues – the colours, shapes, the insides and the outside, the dials and cogs and grease and rust. The work takes apart and throws into disarray, but does it also produce a disintegration that is not a challenge to the status quo but another iteration of the asset-stripping power of capital? When is the disruption of the normative landscape a critical act and when is it a function of neo-liberalism? It is increasingly hard to tell.

The end of the long post-war boom in Europe and the United States in the early 1970s was accompanied, not coincidentally, by the emergence of various forms of cultural nostalgia. A preoccupation with the recent past has, for nearly fifty years, been the defining mode of cultural production in the increasingly post-industrial countries of Europe and North America. The mining of cultural memory has taken numerous forms, including the pastiche and ironic citation of postmodernism, the establishment of academic fields in trauma and memory studies, the perpetual recycling, repurposing and remixing of past styles and forms in music, fashion, architecture and design, the torrent of remakes, reboots and sequels in film, and the recuperation of economically and socially gutted neighbourhoods by waves of gentrification.[6]

There is nothing new about a desire to make sense of the past, but what is distinctive about much of the cultural work conducted since the 1970s is its focus on the individual, either through an emphasis on categories such as memory (rather than, say, history) and affect (rather than, say, cognition or reason). While this attention to the experiential is often intended as a corrective to the exclusionary limits of positivist, 'objective' or official histories, allowing for serious consideration of subjugated, excluded or otherwise under- or unrepresented constituencies, the culture of memory and affect has, in a range of areas, been comfortably accommodated into the biopolitics of neo-liberalism.

The example of gentrification indicates how an aesthetic attachment to the purported authenticity of old things, including places, has become an integral aspect of the exploitation and marketization of the previously forgotten, discarded or derelict. What has also become clear over the last ten years or so is how once radical challenges to revanchist urbanism and environmental despoliation have also become absorbed into the gentrification of the imagination. Strategies of resistance like the Situationist notion of psychogeography have been gutted of their destabilizing critical function and rebranded as a mode of affect tourism. Abandoned post-industrial zones have become the playground for modern ruin aficionados and so-called urban explorers; decommissioned military sites are now prime locations for meditative art films and installations, as well as, in some cases, preserved as heritage and tourist attractions.

The aim here is not to reject engagement with the past but to explore and challenge what has sometimes become an all too comfortable commodification of the strategies of the twentieth-century avant-garde as the cultural wing of neo-liberal spatial politics. The recent preoccupation with, for example, so-called edge-lands, industrial and military sites, both revives and intensifies a long-standing sense of marginal or ignored areas as spaces of critical potentiality. Yet the efficiency with which complex, awkward or resistant ideas and narratives can become repurposed as advertisements for regeneration projects and style options means that questions surrounding the preservation, renovation and appropriation of the material and immaterial remains of the past have become, in multiple different ways, a persistent and urgent issue.

Is 'ruin porn' an appropriately derisory term for the deluge of images of urban dereliction that reached its high-water mark in the years after the financial crisis of 2008, a descriptor that correctly describes a predatory visual culture or a means of dismissing a mode of explorative visual accounting that might have more serious political intentions? What do we make of 'hauntology', a term skimmed off Derrida's *Spectres of Marx* and, for a while, dusted over countless TV, film, literary, musical and photographic projects? Is this an aesthetics of exhaustion given a fashionable distressed rinse or a means of thinking through how to resist the fast fashion strategy of rendering the past as redundant? What can be learned from the tendency, during the 1990s and beyond, to rescue films and TV shows produced in the 1970s that were themselves nostalgic for an imagined enchanted Edwardian England of hedgerows and rustic mysticism, as the raw materials for a new modality of so-called weird folk that combined childhood memories of BBC public information films, Cold War dread, hand-knitted sweaters and library music?[7] Is this asset stripping, a protracted form of mourning, or a serious mode of cultural enquiry?

While artists and writers poked around in the ruins of modernity, in Britain and the U.S. another mode of backward-looking rhetoric, untroubled by the delirium of the hipster *dérive*, gained ground to 'take our country back' and 'make America great again'. The power of right-wing nostalgia, which functioned during the Reagan–Thatcher years as socially conservative cover for neo-liberal economic restructuring and has now flowered into a toxic dream of restorative nationalism, has patently ridden roughshod over what is often disparagingly called the cultural Left. The softening of avant-garde ideas and practices into what can quickly become a mode of picturesque melancholy is unlikely to provide the resources needed to resist an efflorescing authoritarianism.

Although this is a book about landscape, the form this takes is as much about time as it is about space. More accurately, it is about the spatialization of time, the ways time might be experienced, apprehended, stretched and shrunk, collapsed, defied or denied. Recent discussions of nostalgia, whether dismissive or emancipatory, invariably and necessarily reflect on issues of loss and abandonment.[8] There are, though, other ways of thinking through how time slips through the fingers.

The folding of the past, indeed multiple pasts, into the present – a general embrace of temporal fluidity – is perhaps why science fiction is often invoked, in exploratory, dystopian or even utopian moments here when the ostensible topic has nothing obviously to do with science fiction. What lies behind this temporal folding is a sense of imposed disjuncture, a consequence of violent forces tearing up the experience of continuity. At other times, the rupture is willed and embraced, a clear rejection of telos, progress and other fantasies of permanence. The struggle for the control of time is a mode of struggle for territory and it is also a battle for meaning and the right to make meaning. The Marxist philosopher Ernst Bloch, reflecting in the early 1930s on the rise of the Nazis in Germany, outlined the ways in which he claimed the Right had stolen the cultural and historical resources of the Left.[9] The resentment and memories of exploitation and struggle, both petty and structural, he believed had been successfully, though perhaps not totally, appropriated and put to use by the forces of reaction, resources that should properly have belonged to the Left. Bloch understood that, at any given moment, different people experience time differently. He called this the experience of non-synchrony or the non-simultaneous; in other words, not everyone is synchronized into a generally agreed notion of the present. For Bloch, this is partly due to differences in age, class and location. An elderly farm labourer, for example, might have an entirely different sense of the present from a young office worker.

While there is a subjective dimension to this non-simultaneity (ideologically out of sync with prevailing norms), there is also, according to Bloch, an objective aspect in terms of, for example, inequalities of income or access to services. Capitalist modernity might define the present as the most advanced mode of economic and social organization available, but this does not account for the totality of contemporary experience. It was the experience of being out of sync, for Bloch, that allowed fascism to mobilize a campaign for the reclamation of a lost, synchronized existence of mythic completeness. Within a single present, according to Bloch, there lie multi-temporal and multi-layered contradictions. The alienation and resentment experienced by the non-synchronous are, for Bloch, not in themselves reactionary, but they are authentic expressions derived from the inequalities of capitalism. The key, he argues, is not to ignore or dismiss these expressions but to rescue them from the Right.

There is, perhaps, an element of Bloch in Mark Fisher's more recent argument about the cultural fascination, especially in the 1990s and after, with lost futures, whether the utopian aspirations of a planned society enshrined in the concrete architecture of post-war housing estates, or in broader socialistic tendencies of British cultural life during the 1950s and 1960s. Fisher's preoccupations are largely aspects of popular culture, but the argument he develops about the haunted present – haunted by the presence of futures not realized, political struggles unresolved, utopias paused or postponed – is a way of refiguring an often debilitating cultural nostalgia as an emancipatory prospect. This is, broadly speaking, Derrida's argument in *Spectres of Marx*, where, writing in the context of the end of the Cold War, Francis Fukuyama's eschatological 'end of history' and early 1990s market triumphalism, Derrida insists on the unfinished Marxist project. For Derrida, the ghost is not the insubstantial sign of the end of something but of the refusal to expire. Indeed, more important than the notion of the ghost, what Derrida rejects in *Spectres* is a unidirectional temporality that assumes, for one time only, the appearance and disappearance of phenomena. Instead, Derrida argues for circuits of repetition and return, for multiple co-existing temporalities, for returns that are for the first time. In the face of a dominant chronological time that would insist that everything past is over, dead and no longer a threat, Derrida poses a critical notion of time, that is, following Shakespeare, out of joint.

Writing from, as it were, the other side of history from Bloch, Hans Ulrich Gumbrecht's reflections on post-war Germany are equally preoccupied, though differently, with questions of temporality, asynchrony, duration and transformation. Gumbrecht writes of the experience of what he calls 'latency' that emerged in Germany once the experience of destruction disappeared.[10] He describes this latency as a sense that something (or someone) is there that cannot be seen, grasped or touched. It is the experience of a material presence that is never located or defined. As an experience of time, it is about anticipating an unfolding of time that does not come, and Gumbrecht associates the feeling, among his generation who grew up in the immediate post-war period, with a desire for release from the burden of the recent past. The end of the post-war period, for Gumbrecht, never seems to come, and he marks the events of the second half of the twentieth century as, in various ways, continuations or shifts in the post-war but never its end. Even the end of the Cold War only moves the 'finishing line' of the post-war; it does not conclude it. Like Vladimir and Estragon in *Waiting for Godot*, a play Gumbrecht takes as emblematic of the post-war state he is describing, 'we had been moving the whole time without making any progress,' he writes, 'without leaving the past behind us. The postwar seemed never-ending.'[11]

Gumbrecht's sense of temporality is different from Bloch's, Fisher's or Derrida's, but there is nevertheless a shared sense that conventional distinctions of past, present and future are no longer adequate to describe the experience of time or to provide an account of history. The question of being able to leave the past behind, so pressing for Gumbrecht's generation, becomes, as he ponders the world his grandchildren will inherit, a world where, because of electronic media, 'nothing can be left behind'. The past, thus conceived, 'will invade their present – as it has already begun to do now, in the form of multiple and endlessly returning waves of nostalgia'. What we are faced with, he suggests, is 'an ever-broadening array of simultaneities'. When nothing can be left behind, each recent past is imposed, in the present, on previously existing and stored pasts, and in this ever-broadening present of the new chronotope there will be a diminished sense of what each "now" – each present – really "is"'. Because of this expanding present, it seems that we are stuck 'in a moment of stagnation'.[12] This is close to Fisher's sense that we are living in a moment of nostalgia for modernity's quest for the new; all we know is an undifferentiated now.

The mood of latency Gumbrecht describes in the years after 1945 he comes to see as the first sign of a new conception of time, the beginning of the end of history as change. By the 1970s, he claims, it became clear, during the discussions over modernity and post-modernity, that a new sense of time had emerged and that what he had thought was a temporary sense of sustained anticipation was in fact a symptom of a collapsed notion of progress. We may not be at the end of history, but Gumbrecht is clear that, as Derrida also notes in his modification of Fukuyama's flamboyant and reductive claim, a certain conception of historical time may indeed have come to an end.

In the light of these challenges to normative notions of temporality and duration, the purpose here is explore the recent preoccupation with ruins, edgelands, psychogeography and other landscape-related cultural work and to think through the prospect of landscape, not as the passive ground upon which struggle takes place, but as the material through which critical conceptions of place and history can be built. There can be no meaningful engagement with the aesthetics of place that does not address directly issues of class and power, and one of the objectives here is to claim back the radicalism of avant-garde strategies that have been all too successfully absorbed into the normative vocabulary of what places are, what (and who) they are for and what they might mean. In other words, I am interested here in histories of place at odds with the gentrification of the imagination.

The chapters are organized by theme but also perform a kind of movement through some of the dominant landscape tropes of the last decade or so: from the countryside, imagined and real, in Chapter One we move through the so-called edgeland in Chapter

Two and into the post-industrial city in Chapter Three. Chapters Four and Five are concerned with things that are there and not there, with modes of spatialized violence: the outside inside spaces of the much fetishized military landscape, and the contested memorial sites of statues and monuments. Each of these topics or sites has, in recent years, become a focus for debates surrounding place and landscape and the subject (and often the location) for a wide range of literary and artistic works. It is not my aim here to provide an exhaustive account of all the works produced on, say, military landscapes, but instead to concentrate on indicative aspects of contemporary literature, art, photography and film, much of which is grounded in and explores various modes of documentary or non-fictional practice. The challenges and limits of the documentary form, and the means by which truth claims are formally and structurally articulated, are integral to the analysis in each case. The recent proliferation of new modes of non-fictional, observational, participatory or situated cultural work is also part of a history with its roots in the twentieth-century avant-garde commitment to a politics of the aesthetic and an attention to the lived experience of everyday life. While the emphasis here is on contemporary engagement with landscape and urbanism, the intention is to situate current works within a deeper history of place-based practice resistant to the colonizing impulses outlined above.

My focus is largely, though not exclusively, British and North American. The context is the unpicking of social democracy as it has unfolded since the 1970s, in the UK with the assault on the post-Second World War settlement begun by Margaret Thatcher's government in 1979, and in the U.S. with the aggressive rollback of the New Deal order inaugurated by Ronald Reagan in 1980. The UK and the U.S. do not hold a monopoly on generating waves of deindustrialization, outsourcing, privatization, union busting and other 'free market' body blows that have massively increased economic inequality, but they have been very good at it. They are also the Allies that crafted perhaps the most elaborate national myths out of their victory in 1945. The Blitz spirit and the Greatest Generation defeated the Nazis, however high the Soviet death toll. Some of the problems with one-line history lessons like this are encountered below.

Recent political events have rendered the much-touted (in the UK) 'special' relationship between Britain and the United States extra-special, insomuch as the two countries achieved in 2016 some sort of right-wing populist synchrony. This is not a book about Brexit and Trump, but it has unavoidably become caught up with some of the battles in the culture wars – about statues as markers of dubious honour; about the nation-state as a marker of self-evident and transtemporal identity; about the meaning of the past and the cultural work (and the damage) it can be made to do. These are not by any means exclusively British and American concerns but are, more broadly, indicators of the unravelling of the post-Second World War global order and the expectations and assumptions that underpinned it. The issues raised here – about the meanings and relative values of places; about claims of authenticity and entitlement; about how the past is remembered, by whom and for what purpose; and about the kinds of critical cultural work that might be done on, in and around those sites – reach far beyond the British and American contexts within which they are approached here.

Nonetheless, when asked, Mike Nelson explained that *The Asset Strippers* was not about Brexit but, he admitted, 'you can't ignore the timing of it and where you're showing.'[13] Brexit might be the most near at hand example of the demise of the post-war consensus; Trump is another. Already, the concerns of the post-1989 world, even the post-9/11 world – the end of history, the war on terror, the endless insinuation of neo-liberal economics into everyday life – seem dated, less urgent than they ought to be. Right-wing populism has managed to bundle these all together. Indifferent to history, comfortable with endless war, willing to provide a perpetual diversionary spectacle while dark money buys up what is left of democratic institutions and finances the incineration of the biosphere, we are right to be properly alarmed and focused on the present. This is a book about the present, however, only by indirection. It digs around mainly at the tail end of the twentieth century and the early years of the twenty-first. You can't, though, as Nelson says, ignore the particulars of time and place. We live, for now, in a world of asset strippers.

1

What Will Become of England?

One of the artefacts displayed in *The Asset Strippers* is a Vicon Acrobat, a high-capacity rake and swathe turner normally attached to the back of a tractor. The four curly-spoked finger wheels of the Acrobat stare out like overlapping spirographed eyes, proudly perched on a double-stacked trestle table. It is the real thing.

Among the singers recorded by pioneering American folklorist Alan Lomax during his time in England in the 1950s was Harry Cox, a Norfolk farm worker with a large repertoire of ballads and broadsides. Lomax spent the 1950s in London working on the eighteen-volume Columbia World Library of Folk and Primitive Music, an ambitious collection of field recordings committed to the preservation of obscure, dying or outmoded musical forms. Harry Cox did not make it on to the volume of the Columbia World Library dedicated to England, but the recordings of Cox made by Lomax and Peter Kennedy, released on record in the early 1960s, place him as an important twentieth-century source of traditional East Anglian music. Like the Vicon Acrobat, the value of Harry Cox lies in his authenticity.[1]

Included in the songs Cox performed for the collectors is one titled 'What Will Become of England?' This is a version of a traditional broadside sometimes known as 'The Working Men of England' or 'Song on the Times' that describes contempt for the

Vicon Acrobat, seen in an installation view of Mike Nelson's
The Asset Strippers, a Tate Britain commission, at Tate Britain, 2019.

starving poor who are treated like dogs by the rich. 'That is the way old England,' sings Cox, 'the working men cast down.' In Cox's abbreviated version of the song, this situation leads to the question of what will become of England 'if things go on this way'? Other versions include a chorus that provides a more strident response: 'So arise you sons of freedom the world is upside down / They treat the poor man as a thief in country and in town'. The radicalism of the mid-nineteenth-century broadside, with its insistence that 'old England must pay us what she owes', has become, by the time of Cox's 1950s performance, a more abstract and melancholy lament.

A sense of loss, Martin Ryle has argued, 'is also a cultural resource', although Raymond Williams reminds us that 'Old England' has been dying out since at least the 1750s.[2] After the Second World War, rural England was made to represent not only that which had been saved from tyranny but that which was now, once again, threatened, this time by post-war planners and modernization. As David Matless makes clear, this narrative of the rural as the antithesis of modernity is largely a fabrication and the very idea of the rural is produced out of its structural relation to the idea of the urban.[3] The idea of the rural as the repository of old ways, though, is a powerful one. Folk revivals, like that of the 1950s and 1960s, are often responses to rapid social change, and recording singers like Cox not only signals a desire to make a connection with a perceived authenticity that lies somewhere out there, outside the contemporary, but a sense, imagined or real, that old voices and old modes of expression are about to disappear.[4] The preservationist impulse, however, also carried with it, as is clear in Cox's song, a critique of rural poverty and an articulation of long-standing grievances. Despite the danger that gathering the remnants of a lost way of life might serve only an emerging metropolitan taste for a reified rusticity, songs like Cox's managed to call forth and make present a history of struggle and defiance that remains live.

The repeated rehearsal of the imminent extinction of Old England, not to mention the reiteration of old modes of social protest in the present, raises a number of questions about the meaning of the rural past, its forms of representation and their relation to contemporary culture and politics. 'What will become of England if we go on this way?' was already an old question when Harry Cox performed the song for the tape recorder over half a century ago. The question is itself a difficult one, since it invites us to consider unchanging circumstances (going on this way) as unacceptable – what will become of us unless things change? Yet the attraction of rural folk culture continues to be its imagined resistance to change, its responsiveness only to seasonal demands and its rejection of modern teleological thinking. There is something of a paradox here, where a demand for change becomes a refrain that is valued mainly because it is unchanging.

How can loss be a cultural resource? How can paying attention to the rural past retain a commitment to the authenticity of experience while avoiding the pitfalls of a fetishized and aestheticized peasant ontology? How might waning or threatened modes of life be made to speak to the conditions and concerns of the contemporary moment without nostalgia? These questions persist in writing on rural England, as we shall see, but they are already present in compelling form in writing and film from the 1960s and '70s that deploys a mixture of documentary and fictional forms.

Beyond Ethnography

Ronald Blythe's celebrated portrait of a Suffolk village, *Akenfield* (1969), gathers the thoughts and experiences of a broad range of country people, particularly in terms of age and class, derived from interviews conducted between 1966 and 1967. At the beginning of the book, Blythe provides the facts and figures (population: 146 males, 152 females), describes the housing stock, lists the inhabitants by name and occupation, and outlines, by tabulating crops and acreage, how agricultural production has increased in the last thirty years. Dividing the testimonies sometimes by occupation (the school, the orchard men) and sometimes, poignantly, by circumstance (the first, and perhaps the most compelling, chapter, 'The Survivors', documents the memories of the generation to come through the First World War), Blythe in most cases provides brief contextual and editorial commentary before giving way to the first-person accounts.[5]

Akenfield is a book about waves of irreversible change. The countryside it describes has become radically depopulated due to cycles of depression and mechanization, and increasingly denuded of variation as a consequence of the industrialization of agriculture. The removal of hedgerows and the use of chemical pesticides and fertilizers has increased yield but flattened and deadened the landscape, and those few young men who remain willing to work the land escape social death every evening and weekend by tearing off in cars and on motorbikes to the nearest town. The villages are now most attractive to commuters and retirees, who bring with them expectations about rural life largely uninformed by first-hand experience. The demand for the accoutrements of rustic living has at least provided a new source of business for the blacksmith, who is prospering due to the clamour for authentic ironwork among cottage and gallery owners.

The success of *Akenfield* on publication was no doubt in part due to a surge of interest in rural life during the 1960s that accompanied the so-called second folk revival of that decade and the rise of interest in what E. P. Thompson called 'history from below'. The significance of Blythe's book should be understood, as Lynn Abrams notes, in the context of other landmark works of social history of the period, such as Richard Hoggart's *The Uses of Literacy* (1957), E. P. Thompson's *The Making of the English Working Class* (1963), W. M. Williams's *A Sociology of an English Village: Gosforth* (1956), and the oral historian George Ewart Evans's own studies of Suffolk, such as *The Horse in the Furrow* (1960) and *The Pattern Under the Plough: Aspects of the Folk-life of East Anglia* (1966). The growing social scientific and popular interest in history from below, however, also left *Akenfield* open, through the 1970s, to criticism of the methods used to record testimony and to charges of dishonesty and the manipulation of data.

In a 1971 article on the need for authenticity of voice in the transcription of oral history, the Marxist historian and founder of the History Workshop movement Raphael Samuel accepts that the 'spoken word can very easily be mutilated when it is taken down in writing' and that 'some distortion is bound to arise' due to the imposition of grammatical forms, the nature of the questions asked and the interests of the writer.[6] The 'very process by which speech is made to sound consecutive', Samuel writes, is bound, 'in some degree, to violate its original integrity'. The writer, therefore, has to guard against 'the temptations to which he is prone'.[7] As an example, Samuel compares a passage from *Akenfield* to another from Ewart Evans's *Where Beards Wag All* (1970) in order to reveal the poise and coherence of Blythe's text against the 'ebb and flow' of Ewart Evans's 'ragged' transcription of speech. Samuel acknowledges that there is 'as much artistry' in the writing of Ewart Evans as there is in Blythe's; the point, for Samuel, is that Ewart Evans is able to 'preserve the texture' and 'convey in words the quality of the original speech'.[8] Samuel proceeds to make methodological recommendations for the emerging field of oral history – avoid the conventions of written prose; make some attempt to convey the cadences of speech; avoid ordering the material; and accept incompletion and incoherence – that are patently not followed by Blythe.

Samuel has little directly to say about the particular limitations of *Akenfield* as oral history, but the issues of inaccuracy and authorial intrusion are taken up in more pointed fashion by Jan Marsh in a review of the second edition of the book in 1972. Marsh complains that Blythe does not make it clear that *Akenfield* is a fictional combination of more than one actual village; he provides the occupation of only 165 villagers out of a total of 298; and the villagers appear to have little to say about family, despite the fact that kinship networks are usually a prominent concern of settled communities.[9] There are 'not enough facts', Marsh writes, to enable the reader to check Blythe's account. Marsh is willing to accept that Blythe is more interested in literature than sociology, yet the fact that the book is well written becomes itself a source of suspicion. 'As one reads', Marsh writes, 'one is beguiled, utterly convinced that the realities of their way of life shine directly through the villagers' tape-recorded conversations.'[10] What gives the game away for Marsh is that all the voices sound the same. The implausible lucidity and eloquence of the villagers suggests that the controlling voice in *Akenfield* is, in the end, Blythe's: it is the village, charges Marsh, 'as Blythe wants it to be presented'.[11] Despite his admirable determination not to shy away from rural poverty and exploitation, Marsh concludes that Blythe's use of documentary methods has produced a literary response 'moulded everywhere by a cheap "mystical" version of pastoral idealism'.[12] It is a harsh assessment, though not entirely unjust: Blythe is prone to eulogize the ineffability of the taciturn villager, as if the refusal or inability to express oneself is a function of some untranslatable spirit of place.

Prompted by the release of Peter Hall's film adaptation of *Akenfield* (of which more below), sociologist Howard Newby returned to the book in 1975. Newby's own fieldwork had been undertaken during the early 1970s in the same area covered by Blythe; indeed, Newby claims to have interviewed some of the same people and got to know others. Annoyed in equal measure by the uncritical reception of the book in the media and among professional sociologists, Newby, like Marsh, praises Blythe's assault on the sentimental vision of the countryside in *Akenfield*'s opening chapter before suggesting, again, as Marsh does, 'a more subtle form of romanticism' at work in the book. What he means is 'the romanticism of the new rural afficianado [*sic*], sensitive to the hardships and privations of the past, but aware also of a sense of loss'.[13] For Newby, it is 'this "but", an undertone of regret, which marks out the uncomprehending observer from one who has personally experienced the conditions which he describes'.[14] Blythe suffers, Newby suggests, 'from many of the delusions which he attributes to the new urban immigrants – a belief in village life as somehow being more meaningful, representing "real values" and generally having stronger "roots" than the more cosmetic and transient existence that passes for life in the towns'.[15] In the end, *Akenfield*'s enormous success can be accounted for, in Newby's view, by the fact that it is 'deep down a very urban book, written for an urban audience' who want to be assured that '[b]eneath the torments of a stricken past and the plastic world of the present, the rural idyll endures'.[16]

Newby grasps that the issue at the core of any assessment of *Akenfield* is authenticity. Here, like Marsh, Newby is frustrated by the factual claims Blythe makes but then confuses (the collapsing of several villages into one fictional place and the selectivity of interviewees bothers Newby as it bothered Marsh), and he is unhappy, *pace* Samuel, about the tidied-up transcription. *Akenfield* is 'clearly not sociology' for Newby but it 'certainly seems to be documentary'. The problem, for Newby, is that the book, 'unfortunately', is not 'unadorned documentary', even though there hardly appears to be 'a single reader who does not believe it to be so'.[17] Rounding on himself, Newby pointedly asks whether these issues matter. 'Is this unease', he wonders, 'a product of my own over-rigid sense of classification rather than the drawbacks of the book?' As academic history and sociology, 'the book must be counted a failure', Newby concludes, but 'if one drops the demand for authenticity then the book still stands as a magnificent piece of writing, full of imaginative insights into life in contemporary Suffolk and lyrically wrought in a manner which few books in the last decade have equalled'.[18] By the time Paul Thompson's influential *The Voice of the Past: Oral History* was published in 1978, the assessment of *Akenfield* voiced by Marsh and Newby had become the standard line. Thompson repeats their criticisms point for point, as well as reiterating Samuel's concern over Blythe's editorial interventions, and concludes that the book 'cut too many corners' and 'cannot be trusted'.[19] However, *Akenfield* was successful, in Thompson's view, 'in popularizing a new form of rural literature, a cross between the interview documentary and the novel' within which 'oral evidence constitutes its real strength'.[20]

The criticisms directed at *Akenfield* during the 1970s reveal as much about the vulnerable status of oral testimony within the social sciences as they do the inadequacies of Blythe's book. The struggle to retain some measure of scholarly credibility within fields unaccustomed to dealing with the unverifiable and unstable materials produced by oral history accounts, to some degree, for the anxious pecking away at the integrity of Blythe's methods. As oral history shifted away from social science and towards cultural history in the 1980s, however, a more confident, less defensive stance towards the gathering and deployment of oral testimony allowed for a recalibration of the reception of works like *Akenfield* and the kind of truths they were capable of articulating.[21] Thompson is right: *Akenfield* is not failed oral history but a new mode of writing that seeks a grounding in first-hand attention to observation and testimony but without illusions about the limits of objectivity. Blythe is self-consciously *writing* and pursuing a form capable of holding in productive tension the awkward, reticent or muted voices around him with the written record (fictional and non-fictional) of place and with his own mediating voice. It is a non-fictional prose form that shares some of the ambitions, as we will see, of film-makers exploring the fold between fiction and documentary during the 1960s and 1970s. The kind of non-fiction Blythe was exploring in *Akenfield* has, over the last twenty years or so, become an increasingly influential mode of prose writing and has significantly informed the UK's so-called new nature writing.[22]

When Blythe contributed a new preface in 1998 for *Akenfield*'s republication, he made plain that the book 'is more the work of a poet than a trained oral historian, a profession I had never heard of when I wrote it'.[23] His only credentials, he explains, were 'that I was native to its situation in nearly every way and had only to listen to hear my own world talking'. The 'thread of autobiography'

LANDSCAPE AS WEAPON

Blythe suggests runs through *Akenfield* confirms Marsh's suspicion that all the voices belong to Blythe in some sense, but how much Blythe is consciously answering his early critics in the 1998 preface is unclear. He does claim that, as someone who was born between the wars, he was 'in a kind of natural conversation with all three generations' who spoke with him in the 1960s, providing an intimacy that allowed him 'to structure their talk . . . in terms such as I myself was experiencing these things, although now with a writer's vision of them'. This is a nuanced account of the composition of *Akenfield* that means to, retrospectively, position the text some distance away from the kind of truth-claims the sociologists and historians of the 1970s insist Blythe fails to substantiate. From the vantage point of the end of the twentieth century, *Akenfield*'s stance towards history and memory seems more sophisticated, less vulnerable to charges of sloppy methodology. Indeed, words like methodology seem out of place here. Blythe knows what he is doing when he explains that 'I was delighted as always with those who bent the rule, dodged the system and who managed to be "different" within the rigidities which the rural communities like to impose. There is no place like the countryside', he concludes archly, 'for the most imaginative – and blatant – non-conformity.'[24] Here, pointy-headed criticisms like Newby's that the book contained 'rather too many colourful eccentrics for a village the size of Akenfield' are gently swatted away even as Blythe outlines a radical, broader claim for the book's *sui generis* awkwardness.[25]

Akenfield's imaginative, blatant non-conformity is here viewed as of a piece with its subject-matter; in other words, place and expression are considered interchangeable in ways that may remain incomprehensible and inaccessible to the positivist mindset that demands (or at least once demanded) objective data-gathering. Here, perhaps, Blythe is aligning himself with the taciturn villagers and what appears to be their ineffable incommunicability. 'There are various ways to describe a time, a place, a condition,' writes Blythe in the 1998 preface. 'One can come to them from outside and say what one saw. Or one can emerge from within a community, as so many rural writers do, and be at a particular moment its indigenous voice.'[26]

The Right Words in the Right Order

The local concerns about the status of data acquired through the transcription of oral testimony now seem outdated, but the broader issue raised by early critics of *Akenfield* remains a live one. The perceived antagonism between the literary and the factual grounds the objections made by Marsh and others. The critics are happy to call *Akenfield* literature and praise it as such, but it cannot be considered as history or social science so long as its literary qualities are allowed to stand. It is tempting to wonder whether a more poorly written book would have been considered better history. In other words, the extent to which *Akenfield* is considered a success as writing determines the degree to which it can be said, in inverse relation, to be an accurate representation of the facts. The better it performs as writing, in short, the more unreliable it is as history. This would indeed be an outmoded concern if it was not the case that the authority – closely linked, as Newby recognized, to issues of authenticity – of writing about 'nature' and the rural environment continues to be challenged as dubiously 'literary'.

Among the British 'new nature writers', so named after a special issue of the literary magazine *Granta* from 2008, Robert Macfarlane is probably the most celebrated stylist. Among the superlatives most commonly used to describe Macfarlane's work ('elegant', 'exquisite', 'erudite' and so on), it is the 'beauty' of the writing that dominates the critical response. Even sceptics such as poet Kathleen Jamie, who, in the *London Review of Books*, lampooned Macfarlane as the 'Lone Enraptured Male' striding out from Cambridge to subdue our 'sometimes difficult land with his civilised lyrical words', has to submit to the 'lovely honeyed prose' of this 'delightful literary company'.[27] Macfarlane, she goes on, is at once 'polite, earnest, erudite and wide-ranging in his interests. It's rather wonderful – like an enchantment on the land.' It would be tempting to read this as a back-handed compliment if the rest of Jamie's review did not assiduously retreat from the criticisms she made in the first half. The germ of doubt is planted, though, and Mark Cocker makes sure to cite Jamie in a more recent criticism of Macfarlane and other 'new nature writers' published in the *New Statesman* in 2015.[28]

To be fair, Cocker's target is not Macfarlane's work as such but the cultural apparatus that has made him 'an establishment guru' akin to Laurens van der Post and John Ruskin. For Cocker, the reason for Macfarlane's popularity (and here he repeats Newby's objection to Blythe) is that the work, like the rest of the new nature writing, is essentially an urban literature for a primarily metropolitan readership. The realities of land use and environmental despoliation, according to Cocker, are inadequately addressed by a genre more interested in 're-enchantment' than realism. What this usually means is 'clothing a landscape in fine writing, both the author's own and that of other historical figures', even when the actual landscape has been denuded of all that might have made it enchanting in the first place. What is worrying, for Cocker, is that nature writing is dangerously close to becoming 'a literature of consolation' that 'distracts us from the truth of our fallen countryside'. What may be just as bad is that writing about nature becomes merely a 'space for us to talk to ourselves about ourselves, with nature relegated to the background as an attractive green wash'. Invoking Emerson in conclusion, Cocker asks, 'what worth there is in words with no real soil at their roots?'[29]

Cocker's challenge was effective enough to prompt a sustained response from Macfarlane in which he outlined, with plentiful examples, the multiple ways in which literary and cultural work is a vital aspect of an effective environmental agenda. More interesting than Macfarlane's upbeat list of environmental initiatives, though, are the terms of Cocker's criticism. These are themselves, to borrow from Macfarlane's lexicon, 'old ways', rooted in the same questions surrounding authenticity that animated conflicts over the folk revivals and the writing of oral history. Cocker relies on some simple binaries to make his argument, not least the opposition between nature and culture and the alignment of these terms with rural versus urban. The 'fine writing' admired by the cultivated urban consumers of the new nature writing, so long as the binaries remain intact, is nothing but the narcissism of the chattering class and has nothing to do with the 'real' countryside.

Cocker is not wrong in detecting a whiff of privilege about the British nature writing enterprise but the mistake here, as with the challenges to *Akenfield*'s literariness, is to associate literature (and, by extension, culture) with the inauthentic. In Macfarlane's case, in particular, the optimism of his outlook in the face of impending global environmental catastrophe, with its romantic insistence on re-enchantment, wonder and the everyday beauty of the right words in the right order, can be hard to swallow. It is a deep but hard to budge cultural convention to associate authenticity with bleak pessimism and optimism with naive and implausible affirmation. To an extent, Macfarlane cannot win. By displaying his wide-ranging knowledge he is too unapologetically a Cambridge academic. Yet the first-hand encounters with environments near and far he describes mark him as a tourist appropriating the otherness of other places to his own imperial vision. Perhaps none of it would matter if the books were not so successful. The same burden afflicted Blythe, as seen in Newby's grudging list of the accolades heaped on the book ('Book of the Month in the United States; serialised by Time-Life').[30] Success as a nature writer is apparently on a par with selling off a national park to a mining company.

It is not necessarily literature as such that is at issue here but rather a scare-quoted 'literariness' that stands as code for good taste. This is, I think, what Cocker's jab at 'fine writing' is about and Macfarlane is, indeed, the enchanter-in-chief. The nub of the new nature writing's conservatism is its largely unreflective connoisseurship, its endless appetite for the crisp and the exquisite, for things in their right place, releasing or containing the right energies at the correct velocity. The critical purr announcing the beauty of Macfarlane's prose is the affirmative klaxon that insists on harmonizing all elements into the drone of the contemporary picturesque. For that is the category that most fittingly captures the apparently effortless grace with which Macfarlane describes the world. Like a wild swimmer, his sentences can take a dip anywhere and perform just as well in choppy or still waters. The result is always beautiful, everything in place, composed. It is this composure, in the end, that bothers Cocker, just as it was the 'tidying up' of the oral testimony that troubled Blythe's critics in the 1970s.

Part of the problem for Macfarlane, perhaps, as was also the case for Blythe, is the level of self-awareness evident in the writing that can come across as overly mannered: the attentiveness to craft and style is at odds with the expectations associated with the purported straightforwardness of non-fiction. The problem is evident in Macfarlane's contribution to the *Granta* anthology. 'On a cold morning last January, I travelled out to the Norfolk Fens to see a ghost,' Macfarlane's essay opens, establishing his M. R. James credentials from the outset.[31] The essay, 'Ghost Species', is an antiquarian ghost story about the pursuit of exquisite remnants left over from an almost vanished age. They will be found in a field. The narrative, about paying a visit to some old farmers, is framed as a journey into an eerie nether zone: 'Entering the Fens always feels like crossing a border into another world.' Macfarlane explains how, after many journeys to faraway places, he has learned, following Thoreau, that the near at hand can offer the greatest adventures. As such, East Anglian locations are dilated in space and time: the north Norfolk coast is a 'martian landscape'; the Suffolk coastline yields up 'the bones of ancient dead' and 'Palaeolithic flint tools' as well as Second World War weapons. Breckland is 'England's Arabia Deserta'. Everything is 'strange'. An 'anthropologist friend' plans to dig up his deceased father's skull and use it as a candleholder once the worms are done with it. None of this, though, is as 'strange' as the Fens themselves. A lesson in land use and etymology follows.

Macfarlane's spirit guide to this strange place is local photographer Justin Partyka, who specializes in images of rural folk with outmoded jobs. He calls them, we are told, 'the forgotten people of the flatlands'. Justin introduces Macfarlane to the ghosts: family farmers Arthur Vincent and Henry Everett, both in their sixties, who allow the travellers to cross their land, and 98-year-old Eric Wortley and his identical fifty-something twin sons, Peter and Stephen. Before reaching the Wortleys, Macfarlane primes the reader with a literary aside. A field 'ploughed into corduroy lines' and a row of ash trees reminds the narrator of interwar writers H. J. Massingham, Adrian Bell and Henry Williamson, all 'anxious at the disappearance of country life'. Bell's best-known book is called *Corduroy* (1930); perhaps it is the word 'corduroy', rather than the fields, that prompts this literary association. The Massingham narrative ends badly, the man's eccentric hatred of ivy leading to a devastating fall on a rusty scythe, sepsis, amputation and death.

'Ghost Species' is an effective exercise in rural hauntology and it marks the territory with a well-signposted outline of its broad and deep literary lineage. It is also not hard to conclude that the old characters Macfarlane and Partyka depict are mainly there to provide a real world alibi for the essay's existence, the hard evidence that authenticates its self-conscious inscription into the tradition it so much seeks to emulate. Old England is still on the verge of extinction, out there somewhere in the alien landscapes that are, strangely, close at hand. The uncanny never gets old.

This is not to say that Macfarlane is wrong to recognize that things are dying out, and there is a significant sense in which it is the entwined fates of language and the countryside that are the proper subject of his work. In the face of criticism like Cocker's, Macfarlane's writing has become, if anything, more defiantly literary. In *Landmarks* (2015), the title itself deliberately embodies the inseparability of land and the writing about it. Here, Macfarlane gathers together thousands of words for landscape, nature and weather, bundling them into nine glossaries, with a blank tenth intended 'for future place-words and the reader's own terms'. *Landmarks*, explains Macfarlane, seeks to celebrate and preserve words that may have fallen into disuse or that have remained hidden in specific locales. The aim has an ethnographic dimension – to gather the 'specialised' terms used every day by 'fishermen, farmers, sailors, scientists, crofters, mountaineers, soldiers, shepherds, walkers and unrecorded ordinary others' – and a literary one. It seemed 'worthwhile', Macfarlane writes, to assemble 'some of this fine-grained and fabulously diverse vocabulary [and release] its poetry back into imaginative circulation'.[32] Given the *Oxford Junior Dictionary*'s gradual removal of words referring to nature and the countryside in order to make way for terms considered more relevant to modern childhood (out went 'almond' in 2007 and in came 'analogue'), *Landmarks* could not be more pertinent, resisting the inexorable 'falling away' of a 'basic literacy of landscape'.[33] Something 'precious' is being lost: 'a kind of word magic, the power that certain terms possess to enchant our relations with time and place'. Macfarlane makes no apologies in his determination to celebrate and defend this language, and the blank tenth glossary stands as a challenge to the reader to join this reclamation of 'a language of the commons'.[34] Taken together, this language, of which the current book is only 'the edge of the shadow of its possible existence', would constitute a 'Counter-Desecration Phrasebook'. Such a 'glossary of enchantment for the whole earth would allow nature to talk back and help us to listen'. It would be grounded in reality and 'keep us from slipping off into abstract space'. It would be 'supplement and ally' to scientific knowledge, helping us to 'keep wonder alive' in our descriptions of nature and to 'provide celebrations of not-quite-knowing, of mystification, of excess'.[35]

The proximity of extinction is never far away in Macfarlane, and in *Landmarks* it is explicitly extended to language. The sense of the relation between a rich and thriving natural environment and a thick, capacious vocabulary is also about a commitment to craft and husbandry. It is about things having the right names and a right word for each thing in its specificity. Just as each tool completes a specific task, each word ought to fit precisely in order to do its job. As such, the cultivation of a complex and accurate

LANDSCAPE AS WEAPON

lexicon seeks to avoid pedantry by appeals to the integrity of the relation between the craftsperson and the materials, the sensitivity of one towards the other governed by a commitment to getting things right. It is here that a certain authoritarianism, an insistence on everything being just right, tips the project into a suffocating preciousness. In 'Ghost Species', we are told that the photographer has taken thousands of images of rural workers, 'all on colour slide film', of which he is 'satisfied' with eighty and 'proud' of two dozen. This hyper-vigilant quality control is presumably meant to stress dedication to craft and an unflinchingly demanding eye. Of course all the images are on slide film: only the analogue authenticity and incomparable richness of information offered by the transparency is good enough for a serious artist.

Macfarlane is sharp enough, though, to politely pre-empt criticism. 'I am wary of the dangers of fetishizing dialect and archaism,' he admits, and does not want to be seen as advocating 'a tyranny of the nominal – a taxonomic need to point and name, with the intent of citing and owning'. It is good to know, after all, that he perceives 'no opposition between precision and mystery, or between naming and not-knowing.'[36]

Nevertheless, the job of gathering and listing does mean that the compilation of glossaries in *Landmarks* seems to have many of the hallmarks of the folk revival. There is the collaborative drive to pull things together from all over; the pleasure in the inventiveness and aptness of a locally derived idiom, a pragmatism of expression; and the urgency that comes with an awareness of impending collapse. Here it is not the extinction of national character feared by those like Cecil Sharp, who marched across the country saving songs and dances from the oblivion caused by industrialization, but a more generalized cataclysm brought about by global climate change and the evisceration of habitat that threatens to gut the biosphere and the culture that draws upon it. The ferocity of criticism Sharp and his generation later faced as patrician vultures feeding on the creativity of the folk is not without foundation, but the counter-argument, that without their condescension much more would have been lost for ever, is also true. Whatever survives may be a bowdlerized fragment of what there once was, but to imagine it might have been otherwise is to step defensively back into the space once occupied by Blythe's positivist critics.

Macfarlane does his best to hedge around the issue of his own desire for the authentic and the really real, but it is pervasive and contaminates the work. It is there in the throwaway comments, such as the photographer's thousands of slides – the overweening sense of micro-managed particularity – and it is also there, inadvertently, every time Macfarlane anticipates criticism, as if he has thought of every objection and has a ready answer to it. What characterizes the Macfarlane project in the end is not an openness to the wild but a corralling of the life-world into a suffocating zone of insufferable poise. This is a world full of expert 'friends' always generous with their time and knowledge. For all the insistence on mystery and strangeness, there is nothing properly alienating in nature once Macfarlane has encountered it. It is, ultimately, nature writing of the most passive-aggressive kind.

Worked to Death

Macfarlane, like Blythe, recognizes that the integrity of representation must inhere in its form; they insist, in their own ways, on tradition and craft. The mediating agency of the writer was the element that troubled Blythe's early critics because they misread his work as a mode of (failed) objective reporting. While

Macfarlane retains an insistence on the ways reality and language are attached to one another, even if his roll call of loquacious labourers (fishermen, farmers, sailors, scientists, crofters and so on) sounds more like a list of suppliers for a farmers' market than the contemporary workforce, it is never a very rude nature that we read in his books, but instead a highly cultivated version, albeit a resolutely analogue one. This residual sense of attachment to the real is important since, if there is to be a ghost haunting us, it must surely be the spectre of authenticity that shadows the idea of the folk.

Here, I think, we need to return to the 1960s and 1970s and return, too, to *Akenfield*, which becomes, through a film adaptation of Blythe's book, a means of repeating differently the question of how the past might be represented in the present.

Suffolk-born Peter Hall contacted Ronald Blythe shortly after *Akenfield* was published, suggesting they make a film based on the book. Blythe produced a twenty-page treatment that drew on elements of the *Akenfield* interviews crafted into a narrative that moved across generations in order to capture the book's concern with elements of continuity and transformation. Set during the day of 'Old' Tom's funeral, the film is focalized through the dead man's grandson, also named Tom, who must decide whether he is going to finally achieve what his grandfather failed to do: leave the village. Old Tom's only experience outside Akenfield was during the First World War; the film delivers as a refrain from various voices throughout the fact that the only other time Tom attempted to leave – in order to find work forty miles away in Newmarket – he was unsuccessful and had to return home. Old Tom is best known for his failure to leave, and the 'boy Tom' is caught between dreams of emigrating to Australia or Canada, or settling down with his schoolteacher girlfriend in Old Tom's tied

Peter Hall's 1974 film *Akenfield* establishes continuity across time by collapsing distance between generations. A sequence of shots cuts between Old Tom as a boy running across a field . . .

cottage. The young man's dilemma is articulated through the voice of Old Tom's memories of village life and the film slips between the 1970s and scenes from Edwardian Akenfield.

Hall and Blythe were interested in shooting a film with as few of the trappings of a conventional feature as possible. Funded by London Weekend Television and the Film Finance Corporation but with Hall retaining full control (he and producer Rex Pyke deferred their fees), shooting took place at weekends over a period of nine months using available light. The extended production schedule allowed the shape and texture of the project to emerge as the cast and crew developed a rapport over time. Aside from the voice-over, delivered by actor and Suffolk native Peter Tuddenham, all the parts were played by local people with no acting experience. Performers were not given lines to learn but presented with situations within which they were encouraged to improvise. As a consequence, despite some awkwardness, the narrative takes on a strange documentary-like quality. As Hall suggested in 1974: 'We were doing something only cinema could do, for the camera had to be there and "at the ready" to catch "life" when it was invented.'[37]

... and his grandson, also Tom, feeling equally trapped,
walking across the same field.

Due to ill health Benjamin Britten could not contribute
the film's music as planned, but the use of Michael Tippett's
Fantasia Concertante on a Theme of Corelli sustained the Suffolk
connection the film was at pains to preserve. This was, as the
title card announces, 'Made by People of Suffolk'. This sense of
collective endeavour linked the film back to the collaborative
voice shaped by Blythe in the book. Though, as we have seen,
Blythe's crafting of oral testimony was the target of criticism,
the film, making no claims to authenticity (catching 'life' when
it was *invented*), managed to convey a powerful sense of both
contemporary and historical reality. Howard Newby, for one,
considered the film more successful than the book, since it
removed what he saw as the 'tone of regret' that betrayed the
book's preference for romance over a confrontation with the
sharp economic and social deprivations of village life. The film, by
contrast, made plain for Newby that it is low wages, poor housing
and lack of opportunities that are driving Tom to leave Akenfield.
Nevertheless, Newby maintains that most of the people who
liked the film, based on responses in the local press, appeared
to come from urban areas, while the farm workers he consulted

'unanimously found it boring and incomprehensible' as well as riddled with errors of fact.[38]

It is hard, in the end, to imagine a representation of rural life that Newby would accept and though his scepticism towards the commodification of the folk is sensible enough, the instincts of *Akenfield* the film, and the book, are tuned to detecting and capturing the rhythms and textures of rural time as it is warped and bent by unpredictable and sometimes cataclysmic socio-economic perturbations. The film is able to stage these shifts by slipping between present and past while holding the physical form of Tom stable as he embodies the downtrodden Edwardian labourer and the restless mid-century descendent. The sense of entrapment in the film is not one of confined spaces but of open ones, and regardless of how far young Tom walks to escape the expectations of his mother, fiancée and employer, the lanes carry him back to the cottage. Old Tom's warning is allowed to reverberate throughout the film, his words a combination of verbatim extracts from the book.

The film draws upon some of the strongest material from the 'Survivors' section of the book. The film has Old Tom explain early on, in the words of Leonard Thompson, the First World War survivor whose testimony opens the book, how the 'village people in Suffolk in my day were worked to death'. This is 'not a figure of speech', Thompson insists in a revealingly reflexive moment, it 'literally happened'. Going to war is figured by Thompson as an escape, even though the villagers carried their rural innocence with them into dark places. Coming across a marquee in the Dardanelles they think of circuses and the village fete, only to find it full of corpses, 'lines and lines of them, with their eyes wide open'. 'I thought of Suffolk,' says Thompson, 'and it seemed a happy place for the first time.'[39] The horrors of the Suffolk countryside may not have been as grotesque as a tent full of bodies, but it is a landscape of constant fear – fear that the weather will prevent the workers from being paid or that the farmer will over-hear a dissenting word. Later in the film, Old Tom is given the words of nineteen-year-old farm worker Brian Newton, who in the book dismisses what he sees as the pointless perfectionism of the old-time labourers: 'we know that the old men had art – because they had damn-all else!'[40]

The pride of the workers in their labour is a strong theme in the book, the men insisting on painstaking attention to detail in all their tasks. Newton sees this as a marker of how far the labour-ers have internalized the need to please their boss, whom Newton is unafraid to call 'emotional and patronising'. Newton wants the kind of contract he would expect as an employee in any other industry. As it is, he complains, the farmer 'wants me to throw my life into his farm'. Newton says, 'He wants to own me.'[41] Another young ploughman, Derek Warren, also tells how the old men criti-cize his work, which they see as an awful falling off of standards. 'The old men will tell you', Warren explains, 'what an interest they took in their tasks – you could call this their main argument. They were brought up on quality work. Now it is quantity work – you've got to cover the ground.'[42] More sympathetically, the 88-year-old farmer John Grout speaks admiringly of the quality work produced by the ploughmen: 'a farmer could walk on a field ploughed by ten different teams and tell which bit was ploughed by which.' This was not just perfectionism for Grout, but in their interests since a farmer might pay a penny an acre more for perfect ploughing or offer free rent for a year. 'The men', Grout concludes, 'worked perfectly to get this, but they also worked perfectly because it was *their* work. It belonged to them. It was theirs.'[43] Not surprisingly, the farmer's reading of the workers' perfectionism is explained, judiciously, as a combination of self-interest and pride in their work for its own sake. Grout's assessment allows for necessity and enough respect in the workers to concede that they were capable of transcending mere pecuniary advancement.

It is possible to see, perhaps, how Newby's criticism of Blythe's residual romanticism is not without foundation, since such a mystical notion of virtuous labour is here allowed some space. Despite Newton's more pointed critique of the farmer's manipulation of their position (one-off inducements and favours are cheaper than contracted rates of pay), it appears, especially when placed alongside Warren's more mature, less angry assessment and Grout's eminently reasonable sense of the combination of labour's financial and moral benefits, immature and defensive. The young are concerned with quantity rather than quality and with the protections that come with the rationalization of their business. This is entirely understandable and yet rubs up against the sense, elsewhere in the book, especially in the accounts of the blacksmiths and wheelwrights, that rural labour is most properly a form of communion with something elemental.

This sense of the ultimate legitimacy of agricultural labour, despite everything *Akenfield* has to say about hardship and poverty, means that, even as they are positioned as exploited by farmers who care not if they live or die, the farm worker is still respected for his perfectionism. The Reverend Gethyn Owen's reading of the situation is perhaps the most measured the book has to offer. Although a wavering furrow would not have mattered, says Owen,

> a straight furrow was all that a man was left with. It was his signature, not only on the field but on life. Yet it seems wrong to me that a man's achievement should be reduced to this. It was a form of bondage if he did but know it.[44]

Of course it is a form of bondage, and it takes an outsider to say it plainly, but *Akenfield* is more in sympathy with the view from the inside, so Owen's assessment sounds somewhat unsympathetic and not in the spirit of things, despite its eminently clear-eyed view. The reason the issue of the 'art' of the plough is important is, I think, because it underpins Blythe's sense of a dignified and authentic, integrated life of work as a mode of expression. Writing is also an aspect of this art of the plough – it is the ploughman's 'signature', says Owen; it is his 'mark,' says Grout. As a form of writing on the land, ploughing marks into the very soil the identity of the workers in ways that the efficiencies and economies of scale achieved by the modern employee have eradicated for ever. Men are no longer worked to death, but the real loss is the care that turned back-breaking labour into a work of art.

This is perhaps too harsh a criticism of *Akenfield*, and the book and film are indeed at pains to keep exploitation and hardship upfront in the narratives. Nevertheless, the unwillingness to more completely challenge the romanticization of agricultural labour and to continue to see in it some analogue for creativity links *Akenfield*, I think, to the broader tendency to associate 'folk' ways or rural living more generally with positive, authentic and vulnerable ways of life from which something might be retrieved.

Happening Here

The use of non-professional actors in *Akenfield* was very much part of the improvised, documentary-inspired *vérité* aesthetic of the 1960s and '70s, as well as making economic sense for independent film-makers. What films of this kind also sought to achieve was an uncanny fusion of past and present, imagining the past as it might have been represented if cameras had been available. History as present on film, especially through depictions of ordinary life that adopted a faux documentary form, belongs in the company of the living history tendency that emerged during the 1960s, along with the revival of fairs and festivals, steam preservation and re-enactment societies. Raphael Samuel identifies this surge of interest in an embodied people's history as part of a longer movement going back to the 1920s but becoming widespread after the Second World War. In part, it marks a rejection of the official written record as the whole story in favour of a more improvised, though often no less diligently researched, attempt to get at the affective experience of the past. Living history, writes Samuel, 'shows no respect for the integrity of either the historical record or the historical event . . . It treats the past as though it was an immediately accessible present [and] blurs the distinction between fact and fiction.' Importantly, for Samuel, living history 'tells us as much about the present as it does about the past' and makes 'flesh-and-blood figures out of fragments'.[45] Like the two-hundred-year-old protest song performed in the local pub, the prospect of recognizing the power of the past in the present, not as a ghostly presence but as a live force, is a distinguishing mark of Blythe's book, Hall's film and a number of other British films they resemble that combine narrative storytelling and rigorous historical re-enactment.

Kevin Brownlow and Andrew Mollo's low-budget, newsreel-inspired fiction of a Nazi-occupied England, *It Happened Here* (1964), for instance, produced impressive results due to inventive editing, but also because of Brownlow and Mollo's obsessive fixation on authentic material details. Humphrey Jennings had used local people in *The Silent Village* (1943), his ferociously powerful tribute to the victims of the Nazi massacre of the inhabitants of the Czech mining village of Lidice, filmed in the Welsh village of Cwmgiedd and reliant upon a powerful documentary sense of place. The transposition of the Lidice events to Wales allowed for a reconstruction of history that served not only to honour the devastated community but to mobilize the people of Cwmgiedd in a terrifying pre-enactment that stages the kind of violent erasure of entire peoples that might come with Allied defeat. Although Brownlow and Mollo's work is not driven by the sense of urgency that permeates *The Silent Village*, what they share with Jennings is an awareness that the conventions of documentary film-making provide the means of generating a disturbing temporal fold. This is already signalled in the title of Brownlow and Mollo's film: the future orientation of the familiar admonition to learn from the past (it could happen here) is presented as an achieved fact, but also as an event that has somehow come to pass without anyone noticing: it happened here. The function of the documentary film as a recording in the present of what will become testimony – in other words, the use of documentary as constructing and ordering a relation among past, present and future – is, in *It Happened Here*, scrambled to produce an uncanny misrecognition. It is ultimately the newsreel style of the film that creates the reality effect, and the fact that the lack of budget meant that Nazi elements had to be surreptitiously positioned in otherwise 'real-life' locations only adds to the verisimilitude.

The desire to get every period detail right also fuelled Brownlow and Mollo's next project, about the seventeenth-century Digger leader Gerrard Winstanley. Although it was David Caute's novel *Comrade Jacob* (1961) that inspired the project, the pair soon abandoned the novelistic source and its religious emphasis after reading Winstanley's original pamphlets in the British Museum. They decided, Brownlow explained, to 'do this properly, absolutely as Winstanley describes it, word for word as he wrote it . . . We wanted to see what would happen if we made an austere, correct, accurate historical film.'[46] To that end, Brownlow and Mollo reproduced period costumes, including borrowed armour from the Tower of London, sourced rare breeds of livestock and recruited members of the Civil War re-enactment society the Sealed Knot to participate in the battle scenes. Only one professional actor was employed, Jerome Willis playing the part of Lord General Fairfax. The effect of having a famous face on site, the directors explained, produced a suitably deferential response in the non-professional cast. Sid Rawle, leader of the London squatters movement and known by British tabloids at the time as the 'king of the hippies', made an effective Ranter.

Peter Watkins worked as an assistant on *It Happened Here* and, more than Brownlow and Mollo, was acutely interested in the way film form engaged with and produced history. In particular, Watkins was interested from the outset in modes of media representation and storytelling and how conventions might be used against themselves in order to produce counter-narratives at odds with mainstream interpretations of events. Watkins had begun to develop these ideas in two amateur films, *The Diary of an Unknown Soldier* (1959), about the First World War, and *The Forgotten Faces* (1961), a film reconstruction of the 1956 Hungarian revolution. Granada Television refused to show *The Forgotten Faces* because it was considered too realistic. The new head of television, music and documentaries at the BBC, Huw Wheldon, however, asked Watkins to make a film.[47] When Wheldon turned down the idea of a drama-documentary on the aftermath of an atomic attack on Britain (later made as *The War Game*), Watkins suggested an adaptation of historian John Prebble's recent study of the Battle of Culloden. This was the last

LANDSCAPE AS WEAPON

pitched battle to take place on British soil, the final confronta-tion near Inverness between Charles Edward Stewart's Jacobite Highlanders and the British army led by William Augustus, Duke of Cumberland, in 1746. Watkins closely followed Prebble's book and used non-professional actors and a hand-held 16mm Arriflex camera to reproduce an anachronistic documentary narrative style akin to the strategies, especially interviews to camera, deployed by Walter Cronkite in the CBS series *You Are Here*. Shot in tight close-up, the Highlanders, some of whom speak only in Gaelic, are photographed from a high angle in order to stress their vulnerability, whereas the Red Coats are shot from a lower angle, exaggerating their stature.

The popularity of *Akenfield* the book is an indication of how far the idea of history from below resonated not only with histor-ians and sociologists but with a general readership. While this popularity made scholars like Newby uneasy, concerned that mainstream success would compromise the efforts of oral histor-ians to maintain standards, the commitment to socialist history by people like Raphael Samuel, whose History Workshop started at Ruskin College, Oxford, in 1967, and grew through the 1970s to include thousands of participants and an influential journal, marked a shift in the perception of what history was and who made it. *Akenfield* was an important part of that surge, and the film adap-tation connected Blythe's work on oral testimony to independent film's concurrent interest in the narrative possibilities of utilizing documentary forms. Peter Hall's approach to *Akenfield* belongs in the company of Brownlow, Mollo and Watkins, with their shared commitment to an economy of production that disperses agency across a mixed cohort of professional and non-professional participants. The close attention to the historical accuracy and authenticity of material details, a characteristic shared by Samuel and the film-makers, is fused with an approach to narrative that is open to contingencies and interventions introduced through the process of filming. This combination of the obsessively realistic with the improvisatory produces a certain kind of reality effect akin to the 'poetic' intervention of a writer like Blythe into the shaping of oral testimony. Unburdened by the expectations of professional historians, films like *Culloden*, *Winstanley* and *Akenfield* could imagine a mode of history informed by an idea of the past but performed in the present. The issues of power, belonging and exploitation that these films explore are patently not just about history and it is the performative, embodied aspect of the narratives that drives this home.

Stolen History

It is not only the blacksmith's new clientele demanding authentic reproduction ironwork for their restored cottages and barns that marks a reawakened interest in the past in *Akenfield*. The influx of commuters and retirees seeking authentic village life also arrive with expectations. By the end of the 1970s, writes Kynan Gentry, there was widespread interest in the idea of 'the local', especially due to the Left's promotion of people's history and community heritage.[48] By the early 1980s, however, the virtues of the past were repurposed by the Right, most notably by Margaret Thatcher's appeal to 'Victorian values' during the election campaign of 1983. What was now increasingly being called heritage became a battleground during the 1980s for the political soul of the people's history. On the Left, attacks on the commodification of the past were launched in Patrick Wright's *On Living in an Old Country* (1985), David Lowenthal's *The Past is a Foreign Country* (1985) and Robert Hewison's *The Heritage*

Industry (1987). Surprisingly, Raphael Samuel took a less critical view and largely embraced the material culture of the heritage industry in *Theatres of Memory* (1994).

Within the contested field of heritage, the tactics used by film-makers like Brownlow, Mollo, Watkins and Hall in the 1960s and '70s had, by the 1980s, become aspects of mainstream living history tourism, including the use of volunteers either to re-enact key historical events or to perform the tasks that once comprised everyday life, and the strict attention to period detail. Hewison called his book the heritage 'industry' as a criticism of the way the past had been commodified, but the notion of a heritage industry soon ceased to be a scornful term and instead provided a new revenue stream for local economies across post-industrial Britain. It is within this repurposed 'history from below' that artist Jeremy Deller staged his re-enactment of the crucial moment in the defeat of organized labour, the battle between members of the National

A contemporary photograph of the police action at Orgreave Coke Works, Yorkshire, on 18 June 1984.

Union of Miners and Thatcher's riot police in a field in Orgreave, South Yorkshire, in June 1984.

The Battle of Orgreave, funded by arts organization Artangel, was organized by Howard Giles, a leading re-enactment planner and former director of English Heritage's Special Events Unit. Although the 1,000 participants who assembled in Orgreave on 18 June 2001 crucially included around two hundred miners and a few police officers involved in the original events and inhabitants of the village, two-thirds of those performing the re-enactment were recruited from other re-enactment groups such as the Wars of the Roses Federation, the Southern Skirmish Association, Britain's oldest American Civil War re-enactment society, and the Sealed Knot, the English Civil War living history organization that had contributed to the battle scenes in *Winstanley*.

Deller did not shy away from the festive recreational aspects of the re-enactment, erecting a marquee to house archival materials, using loudspeakers to play pop hits from the 1980s and to provide commentary on the action for spectators. As Alex Farquharson explained in a review for *Frieze* magazine, the re-enactment managed to combine 'the innocence of the village fête with an English Heritage event' while sustaining an urgent sense of 'real life' by providing space for 'the deep, unresolved feelings of original participants towards others taking part on the wrong side of the conflict'. For some, Farquharson writes, this 'was more flashback than re-enactment'.[49]

Much as Watkins used TV reportage techniques to challenge the conventional interpretation of the Battle of Culloden, Deller is concerned to use 'living history' to contest the sequence of events as reported at the time by the BBC. A subsequent study by the Broadcasting Research Unit (BRU) found that between June and August 1984, the BBC increasingly reported violence on picket lines, while ITV coverage of violence declined. In a comparative analysis of BBC and ITV evening news of 18 June, the BRU noted a significant contrast in the language and imagery used by the two channels, with the BBC emphasizing pickets attacking police officers. Eyewitness accounts of events contradicted television coverage of Orgreave. Both the BBC and ITV narrative presented the mounted charge against the pickets coming after an escalation of violence, while eyewitnesses insisted that the police charge came before the violence escalated.[50] Making the mounted charge a focus of the re-enactment, Deller therefore sought to restage the historical encounter with a view to rectifying and challenging the official narrative of events. The aim here is not to repeat a secure and stable notion of the past, but to revisit events from a different point of view.

This, of course, is largely the intention of many re-enactment events and organizations, which are not concerned with the slavish repetition of secure matters of fact but with the affective and embodied responses of participants engaged in an ongoing consideration of a sequence of events. Filmed by Mike Figgis, a Hollywood director from the northeast of England with an early background in experimental theatre (he was a member of the People Show in the 1960s), *The Battle of Orgreave* is mindful of its hybrid position as theatre and artwork, living history (a term popular with Deller in his discussions of the project) and performance, authentic engagement and knowing gesture. A book published about the event, *The English Civil War, Part II: Personal Accounts of the 1984–85 Miners' Strike* (2001), includes transcribed oral testimony (and a CD of interviews) as well as ephemera, clippings and short essays from participants and organizers of the re-enactment. A review of the book in the journal *Oral History* is critical of Deller's tendency to pursue the story he wants to tell about the strike at the expense of alternative viewpoints, but, as with the critics of *Akenfield*, this desire for an observer more distanced from the politics of the material mistakes a complex artwork for a 'straightforward' oral history.[51] What Watkins, in particular, makes clear is that there is always a position – that the form produces and shapes the facts.

The Battle of Orgreave shares with *Akenfield* and other works discussed here a commitment to the documentation of social conflict and the representation of voices and stories rarely heard. Deller deploys the devices and techniques of oral history and documentary, as does Blythe, though the aim is to push beyond the reality effects achieved through these conventions in order to critically reflect upon the production of truth. The outcome is work that is participatory and collaborative – it insists upon the veracity of the voices and experiences it gathers together – without claiming to be unmediated. Without fetishizing authenticity, it seeks to cleave to the real while remaining reflexively aware of its own artifice. It is no longer history from below, because it has rendered suspect the hierarchy between subject and object. At its best, it is art.

2

Dreary Secrets of the Universe

American artist Robert Smithson's essay 'The Monuments of Passaic', published in *Artforum* in December 1967, is an account of a bus trip he took to his home town in industrial New Jersey from nearby New York City. The essay combines the conventions of the guidebook, travel article, diary entry and field trip, precisely recording the details of the journey ('On Saturday, September 30, 1967, I went to the Port Authority Building on 41st Street and 8th Avenue') and anecdotal observation ('My eyes stumbled over the news print') in ways that situate the text as at once a careful itinerary and a subjective response to the surroundings.[1] The position Smithson's narrative occupies, though, is most clearly announced by the reading matter he picks up for the journey: a copy of the *New York Times* and a paperback copy of *Earthworks* by British science-fiction author Brian Aldiss. This is a tour that reads landscape through the dual focus of the newspaper and science fiction, an estranged dailiness that fuses reportage with hallucinatory affect. It is also funny, though it can be hard to tell quite how: 'Has Passaic replaced Rome as the Eternal City?'[2] To accompany the text, Smithson includes a number of shots taken with his Instamatic camera that depict unremarkable scenes along the way: the walkway of a bridge, a pumping derrick, outlet pipes and a sand box. These are the monuments of Passaic.

Smithson's essay is, in part, a parody of magazine journalism, especially in its simultaneously offhand and overcooked descriptions. The sky in a newspaper reproduction of Samuel Morse's *Allegorical Landscape*, for example, is described as 'a subtle newsprint grey, and the clouds resembled sensitive stains of sweat reminiscent of a famous Yugoslav water-colorist whose name I have forgotten'.[3] The pedantic and delirious tone Smithson adopts in the essay, with its mixture of familiarity and mild condescension, turns on an unresolved antagonism between an aloof positivism and a narcissistic solipsism. The double-voiced essay at once insists on the literalness of the found object as uncoded event (the bridge, derrick, pipe and so on) and the fact that the identification of such objects and events as in any way significant (including the bridge, derricks and the rest within the category of art by declaring them monuments) is embedded in the procedures and activities of everyday life. The monuments of Passaic, then, are 'found' through overlapping physical, phenomenological, cognitive and interpretive responses to the environment, broadly conceived – not merely environment as 'out there' but, crucially, as an out there always already informed by experience, memory, narrative, modes of perception, ideas, obsessions and preconceptions and so on. The written text of 'Monuments' delivers a Passaic utterly mediated through Smithson's private and professional preoccupations (a scripted interiority) while the photographs, even as they confirm and supplement the discriminating agency of the subject, also pull away to insist upon themselves as depictions of a dumb world of objects: the news from out there is that it is mostly wasteland.

In 1979, when 'Monuments' was reprinted in the first collection of Smithson's writings, it was retitled 'A Tour of the Monuments of

LANDSCAPE AS WEAPON

Passaic, New Jersey', a modification that underscores the procedural aspect of the essay. The new title brings the essay more closely into alignment with the draft Smithson had outlined in a notebook prior to the trip (titled 'A Guide to the Monuments of Passaic, New Jersey') and which, as Ann Reynolds explains, he used to structure both the itinerary and the material he gathered.[4] The impression the *Artforum* article gives of improvised response conceals the partially prescripted nature of Smithson's exploration of Passaic. Smithson further departs from the procedural model by delivering an account of the procedure as it apparently unfolds, the record of places and actions layered with affective responses. Smithson's essay is at once guide and tour, a set of instructions (future-oriented), a following through of those instructions (present) and a record of what happened (recollection). The dilated and contracted temporalities Smithson discusses in the essay (Passaic as the ruin of the future, a 'prehistoric Machine Age'; the suburb existing 'without a rational past') are also immanent in the text, which is scripted, performed and reported back at the same time.[5]

Part of the reason Smithson frames his essay as a guided tour is that Passaic is in the process of becoming a relic of the industrial age. By 1967 Passaic is no longer a busy textile town and the evidence of its industrial past is being demolished. The last train pulled into Passaic in 1963, though the long scar of railroad tracks was not finally removed until the early 1970s. Smithson walks the line, which is functioning as a parking lot, though the incision continues to serve, as it always had, as a means of bifurcating the town: 'The monumental parking lot divided the city in half, turning it into a mirror and a reflection – but the mirror kept changing places with the reflection. One never knew what side of the mirror one was on.' There is no trace of human life in Smithson's Passaic, the crowded tenements and factories replaced with inert, monumental vacancy. The parking lot as mirror is not '*interesting* or even strange', but it does echo 'a kind of cliché idea of infinity; perhaps the "secrets of the universe" are just as pedestrian – not to say dreary'. The site is 'wrapped in blandness and littered with shiny cars', their 'indifferent backs' reflecting the 'stale afternoon sun. I took a few listless, entropic snapshots of that lustrous moment. If the future is "out of date" and "old fashioned," then I had been in the future.' In the middle of its first push towards urban renewal, Passaic in 1967 is the hinge between past and future. The congested, blackened streets have given way to a bland and 'sunny nebulosity', a future of parked cars that already, in its redundancy, seems old.[6]

The folding of old Passaic into the new is not yet achieved; Smithson catches the town as it shifts into post-industrial uniformity, a moment when the remains of the old order are still evident. A new highway is being constructed alongside the old River Drive and it is 'hard to tell the new highway from the old road; they were both confounded into a unitary chaos'. In the town at the weekend, the process of transformation is arrested, and it is this suspension that contributes to the peculiar stillness Smithson encounters: 'Since it was Saturday, many machines were not working, and this caused them to resemble prehistoric creatures trapped in the mud, or, better, extinct machines – mechanical dinosaurs stripped of their skin. On the edge of this prehistoric Machine Age were pre- and post-World War II suburban houses. The houses mirrored themselves into colorlessness.'[7]

Edges

Smithson's short essay anticipates a number of themes and strategies that become commonplace in a good deal of late

twentieth-century writing about place. It is deliberately deflationary, self-reflexive, adept at appropriating, through mimicry and
parody, conventional modes of address, folding observational data
into psychological reverie; it stresses the encounter, the apparent
unstructured nature of the walk, the discovery. The process of
working through the space is never naive or innocent, however;
instead, moving through space is mediated by literary, art historical and other assorted cultural references and allusions: the
phenomenological encounter is always also a reading process and
a citational practice. The essay does not refer to, but draws upon,
writing about urban wandering that stretches back to at least Poe
and Baudelaire, and is a close relation to surrealist works such as
Louis Aragon's *Paris Peasant* (1926) and the Situationist *dérive*.
'The Monuments of Passaic' is also, crucially, a document of the
emerging post-industrial landscape, of dereliction and upheaval,
of erasure and abandonment.

As his reference to Aldiss suggests, Smithson was a fan of
science fiction, and it is no surprise to find that J. G. Ballard is
another prominent source in Smithson's writing. Ballard was
part of the generation of Europeans obsessed with the monstrous
excesses of the United States, in equal measure aroused and
repulsed by America's indifference to history and willingness to
bulldoze the present to make space for new realities. The vision
of flyovers and high rises Ballard injected into British culture is
an overcast, rain-soaked version of the futurist concrete paradise
architecture critic Reyner Banham celebrated in Los Angeles.
Smithson's encounter with the new highway cutting through the
landscape (the river had to be diverted) perceives the radical
disruption of time and space such construction projects introduce
and, like Ballard, he is fascinated by the psychological, as well
as the physical, consequences of infrastructure developments

that reshape the human subject in relation to technology and the economy. What Smithson outlines in 'The Monuments of Passaic' is a poetics of space commensurate with the coming post-industrial condition in Europe and the u.s.

Others have sought to craft a vocabulary of dereliction sharp enough to convey the layered significance the broken-down hinterland is seen to hold. In the 1990s, for example, Spanish architect Ignasi de Solà-Morales suggested the term 'terrain vague' to describe empty or abandoned spaces. The French *terrain*, he explains, has a more urban quality than the English *land*, while *vague* carries with it the oscillation and instability of the German *Woge*, or sea swell (also present in the French *vague* as *wave*), as well as the English words *vacant*, *vacuum* and *vague* (as in indeterminate or imprecise).[8] For Solà-Morales, the areas he has in mind are, precisely because they are uninhabited, unsafe and unproductive, spaces of potentiality and refuge from an instrumentalized and overbearing urban culture. The *terrains vagues* are, he writes, 'foreign to the urban system, mentally exterior in the physical interior of the city, its negative image, as much a critique as a possible alternative'.[9] A similar recognition of the possibilities abandoned or ignored sites offer is noted by urban designer Alan Berger, whose survey of American wasted landscapes adopts another neologism, *drosscape*, to describe what he called the spaces 'within urbanised areas that eternally elude the overly controlled parameters and the scripted programming elements that designers are charged with creating and accommodating in their projects'.[10]

In 2002 environmentalist Marion Shoard offered a British take on the terrain vague in an essay she called, simply, 'Edgelands'. Reflecting on the status of waste sites, scrapyards and warehouses, big box stores and disused industrial areas, office parks, golf courses, allotments and other ragged and undefined spaces, for Shoard what is most striking about the edge between settlement and countryside is not its novelty but its massive contemporary size and complexity. No longer simply a fringe or strip at the edge of town, the edgeland is now a vast 'interfacial rim' that has taken on its own character and where, despite a degree of abandonment, 'huge numbers of people now spend much of their time living, working or moving within or through it'.[11] The edgeland, for Shoard, is not so much the post-industrial desert appropriate for episodes of Ballardian anomic reverie, but instead a thriving, if often toxic, economic and social enterprise zone. Despite its apparent usefulness, though, Shoard concedes that the edgeland is rarely attractive and such places are 'nakedly functional, desolate, forsaken and unconnected even to their own elements'. Still, as Smithson knew, these were precisely the qualities that were most characteristic of the achievements of advanced capitalist societies and, as such, looked at the right way, perversely marvellous, even monumental.

Resisting the emancipatory possibilities implied by Solà-Morales and Berger, Shoard nonetheless identifies in the unruliness of the edgeland a subversive spirit of play that makes such places attractive to children and wildlife (and, we might add, writers and artists). As an edge, such areas invariably operate as frontier zones and are frequently used as dumping grounds, experimental sites for extra-legal enterprise and dodgy deals, and improvisational spaces for anything unsightly or outside conventional acceptability. Edgelands also, for Shoard, precisely because they are unmanaged and unnoticed, 'more accurately express the character of our time' than more publicly minded spaces.[12] The sheds and substations, sewage farms and breakers yards are the reality of our economy and our society.

Poets Michael Symmons Roberts and Paul Farley happily claimed the term 'edgeland' for their 2011 book, a series of reflections that sought to flesh out some of the possibilities implicit in Shoard's essay. The chapters are called things like 'Cars', 'Paths', 'Dens', 'Containers', 'Landfill', 'Sewerage'. Loyal to childhood memories of unsupervised adventures among the scrubland at the back of estates, *Edgelands* reaches for a kind of offhand lyricism but more often reads as if it has been scripted for afternoon radio. In the chapter on cars, for instance, Farley and Roberts write that 'maybe, because we put so much of ourselves into our cars, maybe we see our own demise foreshadowed in theirs, our own future, cannibalised for parts, broken open, cast aside.'[13] That Ballard probably coughed up furballs sharper than this is an indication of the limits of the edgeland as zone of transgression.

One of the problems with vacant spaces, as Solà-Morales warned back in 1995, is that once identified, their radical potential can too easily be cancelled, as they are absorbed back into the conventional flows of the city. All too often, he writes, when 'architecture and urban design project their desire' onto a terrain vague, 'violent transformations' are the result. Estrangement is converted into citizenship, he warns, and 'the uncontaminated magic of the obsolete' is dissolved 'in the realism of efficacy'.[14] As in Symmons Roberts and Farley, a fairly upfront romanticism animates the sense that the space of possibility is forever on the threshold of being hammered into conformity. Solà-Morales wants to resist planning and efficiency by tapping into more organic 'flows, the energies, the rhythms established by the passing of time and the loss of limits', but such an appeal is not without dangers of its own.[15] Among them is the lukewarm mellow fruitfulness of the post-industrial sunset, a soft-focus version of Allen Ginsberg's 'hilly tincan evening sitdown vision'.[16]

LANDSCAPE AS WEAPON

Problems of complicity dangerously threaten to undermine the aesthetics of the edgeland and even Iain Sinclair, the godfather of British literary landfill poetics, is not immune from the charge. In a review of Sinclair's retread of poet John Clare's 1841 eighty-mile march home from High Beach Asylum in *Edge of the Orison* (2005), Robert Macfarlane asks whether Sinclair's obsessive tracking of power in Britain is a form of resistance or nothing more than a 'document of nostalgic radicalism'.[17] Sinclair's sensibility, writes Macfarlane, sometimes seems to be one more 'usually associated with the *Daily Telegraph* [rather] than with avant-garde psychogeographers'. John Heartfield, writing in *Blueprint* magazine in 2004, similarly rejects the backward-looking antiquarianism of Sinclair, Peter Ackroyd and Michael Moorcock as a depoliticized Situationist psychogeography, overly concerned with the mythic and the occult. Sinclair's interest in East End gangsters and other colourful cockneys appeals mainly, Heartfield goes on, 'to gentrified urbanites looking for local colour' and is attractive mainly because it marks 'the passing of a way of life'. What has passed, according to Heartfield, is the world of work and London's working class has migrated out of the city to Hertfordshire and Essex, replaced by 'new, gentrified Londoners who are the natural audience for Londonostalgia'. Wandering without purpose, for Heartfield, 'is the privilege of a leisure class'.[18]

Sinclair is not unaware of the problems and, as David James notes, there is a strong self-satirizing element to Sinclair's later work that is partly an attempt to destabilize and deflate the occult claims made in his books in relation to place.[19] Heartfield's criticisms seem more aimed at Sinclair's readers than the work itself, and while Sinclair has been successful in finding – indeed, creating – a mainstream readership for what started out as a fairly recondite project, the gentrification of psychogeography probably has more to do with broader cultural trends than with the work of an individual author. The general point Heartfield makes, though, is an old but pertinent one: how can a critical engagement with the past avoid contributing to the commodification of its subject? This is not really Macfarlane's beef with Sinclair, though he does worry that something has become detached from the present and that the radical implications of Sinclair's practice may have unravelled into a mere inventory of curmudgeonly grievances. Nonetheless, without Sinclair's presiding influence, it is hard to imagine what a British edgeland aesthetic would be like. It is Sinclair's work, combined with that of writers like Richard Mabey, whose *The Unofficial Countryside* (1973) is another edgeland lodestar, that gives Macfarlane and other 'new' nature writers their distinctive vantage point on the contemporary landscape, a prospect informed as much by Tarkovsky and Ballard, or by M. R. James or H. G. Wells, as by William Cobbett or Richard Jeffries. The presence of Sinclair, including the occult ambience and Left nostalgia, runs deep in contemporary British writing about place.

Sinclair staked out his territory a long time ago, in the roiling emergence of neo-liberalism during the 1960s and '70s. The retooling of London (and its extensions) by the Right and the city's grimy refusal to go all the way gives him form and content, source and outcome. The writing is derived from a ground-level encounter with the dailiness of place, but this empiricism is fed through a consciousness routed by way of William Blake, Guy Debord and Black Mountain College. As prose, the result is maximalist, digressive and, by turns, deflationary and flamboyant, arch and demotic. Often structured around expeditions out into the ragged pointlessness of the contemporary British landscape, the uncovering (or inventing, the effect is similar) of circuits of influence and relation among disparate social, political, temporal, geographical and historical elements, the work is all about the journey. There are more stories in Sinclair's London than any of us, including Sinclair, knows what to do with, but the point is immersion and overkill, not order. If there is an order it slowly leaks out of the prose as it gnaws at the edge of a crossroads of possibility.

The political point of this is to break the chokehold of official narratives and the overlaid pathways of conventional spatial management. Out of the furrow, in Situationist fashion, walking the wrong way, aslant, riffing on the found objects, the unsuspecting bystanders providing the kind of one-liners that would never ring true if they were made up. Macfarlane's journeys, like *Blue Peter* expeditions, are full of his friends, helpmates on standby with expert situational knowledge, ready to repopulate the countryside with a new kind of folk wisdom hybridized from environmental scientists and reskilled artisanal types with a penchant for open fires. Sinclair has been doing this longer and with a stronger sense of irony. His companions and spirit guides are more likely to be losers, market traders and low-end gangsters: more London Weekend Television than BBC.

What Sinclair has taught his followers more than anything, though they have learned with differing degrees of success, is that the everyday can be supercharged with significance; that the relation between being there and writing about it is labile and open to all sorts of interesting creative abuse. For all the dangers of complicity, the re-enchantment of the world is important business if done well. The gap between fiction and non-fiction is of little concern to Sinclair, since it is the linguistic embodiment of the encounter that counts. This is where Sinclair and Macfarlane distinguish themselves in relation to their many followers: the writing must always be sufficient. It is for this reason, from a literary point of view, that the edgeland is important. The more ordinary the place, the more powerful the literary magic has to be to persuade us to keep reading. The demand for the re-enchantment of the landscape, if it is to mean anything, must be met in the most grimly unprepossessing places. Anyone can do the Cotswolds, but what about a roundabout near Southend? You need a real writer for that.

Out of Sinclair's many adventures, it is therefore *London Orbital* (2002), his pedestrian exploration of the M25, the motorway that encircles the capital like a 'rage-inducing asteroid belt', that most properly tests his mettle as a writer about place since here he is confronted with perhaps the most Ballardian landscape in the country.[20] The motorik nihilism of the M25 does not only bewitch Sinclair but it prompted his film-maker associate Chris Petit to collaborate with the writer on a follow-up film essay, also called *London Orbital* (2002); in a project concerned in no small part with repetition, changing the title would be going too far. Unlike the book, which is about walking where you are not supposed to walk, the film is about driving, the only thing you are supposed to do on the motorway. Joe Moran is right, though, when he notes that the conventional celebration of speed and open vistas associated with driving is not exactly what happens on the M25, which, although it cuts through the Green Belt and conservation areas, provides little in the way of distinctive visual reference points. Earth mounds and a screen of trees prevents the motorist from seeing much at all; driving the M25, Moran claims, 'is about as visually stimulating as moving through a tunnel'.[21] What is worse is that, since planners underestimated traffic flows, the Orbital was obsolete at the point of completion. Petit's film embraces rather than resists this unpromising environment and becomes a meditation on boredom and low-level irritation. The ambient

'The road becomes a tunneled landscape, a perfect kind of amnesia'
in Chris Petit and Iain Sinclair's 2002 film *London Orbital*.

sound from the radio of traffic reports and a phone-in about the
M25, full of complaints about congestion and dangerous driving,
punctuate Petit and Sinclair discussing motorways.

At this juncture, edgeland discourse has perhaps reached a
point of bathetic deflation that leaves it unprotected from the
charge of self-parody. This is not the transgressive space hoped
for by Solà-Morales and others, but the zone of a particular brand
of British middlebrow comedy made by self-lacerating middle-
aged white men. Yet it is here, in the punctured radicalism of
the road movie that goes nowhere, that Petit and Sinclair do
seem to have grasped the point of the edgeland, so vividly and
concisely reported by Smithson, as the space of slow collapse –
the devolution of empire, ambition and efficient purposefulness.
For Smithson, the contemporary version of Rome might be
Passaic; for Sinclair, the new Passaic is somewhere like Grays in
Essex, where 'laughable attempts at civic revival . . . do nothing
to diminish the galloping entropy'.[22]

The Neat Old Deserted Stuff

The metaphorical heft of the edgeland is powerfully seductive, providing, for some, an emancipatory space akin to bohemian enclaves before gentrification and a space of resistance from the reductive binary logic of urban and rural. The 'vague' aspect, the hybrid, liminal, non-instrumental, playful, improvised – all the positive valences of a notionally 'creative' zone of potential liveliness – are there in the shitholes between the fields and the streets. Even the often literal toxicity of edgelands provides scope for libertarian tropes since, free from regulation, wild species flourish there.[23]

The other side of the edgeland – its productive aspect – stands at odds with the romantic reading of the edge as liminal possibility. From this viewpoint the edgeland's precarious position, in relation to the valorized rurality of the countryside (the 'official' countryside that is the visually presentable face of the national landscape) and the glorified authenticity of the urban, is that it is, as Shoard knew, the ugly reality of capitalism. If the financial core of the city comprises the sleek, aggressive hard surfaces providing the frictionless circulations of the stock market, the edgeland is the all too material sludge plain of broken-down or artificially durable rubbish and the low-end retail environment of the drearily cost-conscious.

The claims made by Shoard and picked up by Farley and Symmons Roberts that the edgeland is a space of aesthetic potential, then, rightly identify the provocatively apposite conditions of the terrain vague as a space that speaks to the contemporary condition. But the narrow range of what constitutes the aesthetic here, and its limited political possibilities, leave this call sounding like a plea for the reorientation of perception, so that the edgeland can be included among the beautiful or the picturesque (*Edgelands* was broadcast on BBC Radio 4). A more demanding consideration of the relationship between aesthetics and politics is required if the edgeland is to serve as more than just a rough-trade version of the loft conversion.

The celebration of the liminal, the hybrid, the improvised and the contingent might serve to establish a protean space of potential in the context of identity formation or in terms of liberty of thought and action. But why should such terms also be considered attractive in places? The indeterminate and unregulated nature of the edgeland as the space to which the state is indifferent does not mean it is free in any sense other than interpretations can be freely placed upon it. Those very terms are also the terms which validate the freedom of the market, the improvisation of the entrepreneur and the contingency of the employee on a zero-hours contract. The liminal might also be the space of homelessness and addiction, of the undocumented migrant or the field or stream unprotected by environmental legislation, the landfill or the fly-tipped roadside. In other words, the language of free play is also the deregulated zone of market freedom – freedom from planning and responsibility, freedom from the kinds of restriction that might harm the environment or people. The slippage of terms used to describe the emancipatory identities and aesthetic practices of edgeland discourse, the ambivalent space where landscape is both an object of aesthetic contemplation and document of domination, is where Sinclair gets closest to the contradictory core of the edgeland's appeal, which can never be made safe for the nostalgia of childhood. Still, the affective pull of the pre-Thatcher world is hard to resist for those of a certain age, especially those whose sensibility was shaped by the punk edgeland aesthetic of the 1970s.

When the music journalist Jon Savage first visited Manchester in 1977, he took a set of photographs of the city that remained unexamined for thirty years. The negatives had been lost but a friend rescued the images from an old contact sheet. In a 2008 article for *Critical Quarterly* titled 'The Things That Aren't There Anymore', Savage uses the photographs to reflect on the changed urban landscape. The rediscovered photographs coincide with Savage returning to Manchester to make a film about Joy Division, the band that, more than any other, have come to embody the glamour, if that is the right word, of late 1970s post-industrial Britain. In good hauntological fashion, Savage uses the emergence of ghost scenes pulled out of the aged emulsion to activate multiple temporalities: 'Many were of the derelict thirties council blocks that surrounded the city's major punk club, the Electric Circus, while others harked back to the nineteenth century: mills and viaducts.'[24] The punk subculture, folded in among the 1930s and the nineteenth century, has become another thing that is not there anymore.

Punk, Savage reminds us, was born out of the collapse of cities both in the U.S. and the UK, caused by white flight and disinvestment, slum clearance and, in Britain, the mess left over from the Blitz: 'Whole districts had been torn down in New York, Manchester, Liverpool and London and, before they could be redeveloped, the money ran out.'[25] As Savage explains elsewhere, swathes of London were still, in the mid-1970s, ragged and abandoned, seeming to embody, he writes, 'an emotional truth: this is what England is *really* like'.[26] This is the truth, already limned in Smithson's New Jersey, where the future is already old, that punks recognized in Ballard's self-described 'inner space' sci-fi of caved-in cities and in David Bowie's and Iggy Pop's Berlin records: the wreckage of modernism's post-war concrete utopia of mass dwelling and automotive liberty. Instead of the despair that most often accompanies decline, punk registered a kind of apocalyptic thrill at the prospect of what, mistakenly, as it turned out, looked like the death of an entire social order.

Discussing the emergence of punk during the summer of 1976, Dick Hebdige notes how the respite from daily reports of economic crisis brought by uncommonly hot weather soon turned into a sense of apocalyptic foreboding. The 'miracle' of the heatwave became, in the media, a 'freak disorder', 'a dreadful, last, unlooked-for factor in Britain's decline'. Drought was declared, grass burned, water was rationed, crops failed: 'Economic categories, cultural and natural phenomena were confounded with more than customary abandon until the drought took on an almost metaphysical significance.' By the end of August, 'excessive heat was threatening the very structure of the nation's houses (cracking the foundations) and the Notting Hill Carnival, traditionally a paradigm of racial harmony, exploded into violence.'[27] The kind of social collapse held back symbolically by the moral authoritarianism promoted during the mid-1970s in endless film and TV police procedurals and vigilante fantasies was here aided and abetted by freak natural intervention.

For the 'young and foolhardy', as Savage puts it, 'there was nothing to lose' under such conditions and cheap accommodation provided a space of possibility as well as an aesthetic and political context for punk. This is the edgeland mythos in full bloom, especially when Savage quotes David Thomas, singer of Cleveland, Ohio band Pere Ubu, who explains that the city he loved 'was the one that everyone else hated'. Cleveland provided a dystopian dreamscape for Thomas: the city 'was totally deserted, people fled when the sun went down. It was run down, but we thought it was beautiful at the time of youth when you're prone to romanticism . . . we felt that we owned it, because nobody else wanted it.'[28]

The sense of possibility Thomas celebrates here, opened up by official disinterest, is foreclosed in a different edit of the interview, however, by a closing remark: 'that's all gone now. The city has become revitalised: they're tearing down all the really neat old deserted stuff and putting up condos.'[29] Only in the inverted bohemian aesthetic typified by Thomas could 'revitalised' be understood as a bad thing; we are back in the realms of the picturesque here, another version of the ruin reverie, the desertion, the contemplation of the rise and fall of civilizations, the romance and the space of a lost past put to use in the present.

Savage recalls Ian Curtis wandering Manchester in search of, as his wife Deborah puts it, 'the places where white people don't usually go'.[30] By 2006, when Savage returns to the city, 'many of the places associated with the group had disappeared so completely that it was hard to pinpoint where they had been ... New apartment blocks sat cheek by jowl with vacant, derelict lots: the streets were often blocked by builders' deliveries.' The 'gleaming new buildings', though, are 'underpinned' by the city's industrial past and just around the corner from the overpriced footballers' bars are 'piles of empty liquor bottles; sex shops; Popular Book Stores selling porn under the counter; junkies shooting up in the open air at the back of the old Smithfield Market'. It is clear that the 'sleaze hadn't been eradicated' and there is a 'curious, edgy quiet' after dark. 'Who lived in all these new flats and how did they earn their money?' he wonders. The redevelopment 'had not succeeded in eradicating the ghosts of the people who had lived there', but the question of what happened to them remains unanswered.[31]

Savage's rediscovered 1977 snaps and evaluation of punk's urban *dérives* confirm the edgeland argument about dereliction providing sites for unregulated interpretation and practice of city space. The tendency to exoticize the underbelly (the places white people do not go), however, persists. The sense of loss and

LANDSCAPE AS WEAPON

a familiar romantic grasping for an irretrievable, though almost palpable, past places Savage's essay squarely within the precincts of the early twenty-first-century discourse of urban melancholy. More critically, though, what Savage also recognizes is how redevelopment has simply pushed sleaze and poverty out of sight and created ghost spaces out of the absent presence of the poor.

As we have seen in relation to the idea of the rural, part of the danger in addressing decline and loss is that these become the characteristics of a picturesque aesthetic of often depopulated abandonment and decrepitude. With punk's appropriation of the negative, Savage's punk lament performs a strange doubling. The decay celebrated in the 1970s as a mode of liberation from fantasies of streamlined modernity is now also among the things lost. The derelict 1930s blocks in Savage's recovered snapshots are now joined by vanished punk rock venues, squats and other hangouts that once marked a territory of resistance. The ghost streets provide the perfect backdrop, though, for documentaries on the old days, which is why Savage is back in Manchester.

Perhaps the rock documentary is among the more appropriate modes in which to address the kind of complicated temporal struggle going on in relation to the allure of the edgeland, whether it be the pre-gentrified 'inner city' or the deregulated post-industrial sludge zones of the not-yet rural. One of the things lost as neighbourhoods are 'reclaimed' for residential and commercial use is the subcultural energy that was once allowed to percolate out of them. The general decline of popular music's cultural importance over the last thirty years (regardless of how many downloads or streams are sold) has been met by the growth of the market in reissues, revivals and expansive critical (and not so critical) reassessments. The rock documentary is therefore a crucial aspect of the new ecology, since it provides context, texture and cultural value to all sorts of old stuff that is now in circulation as part of popular music's perpetual present. Joy Division are a twenty-first-century global brand and stories about where the Electric Circus used to be are part of the fabric of a rock pantheon as fiercely guarded as any tradition that T. S. Eliot might have defended.

At its best, the rock documentary can do serious cultural work in relation to place and politics because, as the superhero comic books have known for a long time, a powerful origin story can drive a compelling narrative out of all proportion to its ostensible subject. Such is the case with Julien Temple's documentary of Essex pub-rockers Dr Feelgood, *Oil City Confidential* (2009), which manages to navigate the same kind of spatio-temporal cracks traversed, under different circumstances and in different places, by Blythe in *Akenfield* and Smithson in 'The Monuments of Passaic'.

Down by the Jetty

Canvey Island distends down into the Thames Estuary, barely above sea level, from the backside of Essex.[32] The southern area of the island has served as a petrochemical shipping and storage facility since the 1930s and was also home to the UK's hard-boiled musical Motor City retreads Dr Feelgood. What Temple does in *Oil City Confidential* is make full use of the cultural inversions required to make sense of the odd situation of an Essex pub band committed to urban African American rhythm and blues. In the portrait of Dr Feelgood and Canvey Island, the extent to which the aural and visual vocabulary of urban American popular culture has become inseparable from, though by no means unin-flected by, British cultural forms is clear. Part of Dr Feelgood's self-mythologizing involved imagining Canvey Island as a mud-caked Oil City and themselves as the Essex version of both a rural underclass (Temple's film includes old photographs of band members in teenage jug bands, where the kids pose deliberately as if they were in 1920s Mississippi) and urban blue-collar bluesmen. The band's name is borrowed from the song 'Doctor Feelgood' originally recorded by Piano Red, a Georgia-born albino African American blues singer who latterly also went by the name Dr Feelgood: white men playing black music with the same name as a white black man.

Dr Feelgood are also often identified as forerunners of punk, their other big influence being the MC5, the Detroit-based garage radicals with whom members of what would become Dr Feelgood shared the bill at the famous London Rock and Roll Show at Wembley Stadium in 1972, and whose manager, John Sinclair, was an active member of the White Panther Party, the radical organization established in response to Black Panther Huey Newton's call for white participation in the fight against racism. The cover of the debut Dr Feelgood album, *Down by the Jetty* (1975), deliberately echoes the design of the first MC5 studio album, *Back in the USA* (1970), with its plain white background framing a grainy monochrome photograph of the band looking ugly. The MC5 top and tail their album with rock and roll standards by African Americans – Little Richard's 'Tutti Frutti' and Chuck Berry's 'Back in the USA' – while Dr Feelgood deliver a version of John Lee Hooker's 'Boom Boom' (written by Hooker while working at the Apex Bar in Detroit) along with Londoners Johnny Kidd and the Pirates' 'Oyeh!' and Southend stalwart Mickey Jubb's 'Cheque Book'. *Down by the Jetty*, then, is a version of Detroit proto-punk that claims a hybrid Thames delta-Motor City blue-collar lineage.

It is this strange convergence of influences that Temple reproduces in *Oil City Confidential*. While there is a healthy irony at work in the Feelgood film's mythologizing, with spliced clips from classic UK noir films like *Night and the City*, *Payroll* and *Robbery* adding comic pace to the story of the band's early days, it is no less a film about industrial collapse and long-disregarded working-class fortitude in the face of structural and environmental inequality. There are moving sequences dealing with the devastation of Canvey Island during the 1953 flood (with echoes of Hurricane Katrina in the suffering experienced by the socially marginalized residents of this ragged outpost of East London) and archive footage of the campaign during the 1970s against the building of more oil refineries that includes an appearance from a long-haired pre-Feelgood Wilko Johnson.

Canvey Island received the first delivery in the world of liquefied natural gas by container ship – the evocatively named *Methane Pioneer* – from Louisiana and later became the subject of an influential assessment on the risks to a population living within the vicinity of petrochemical shipping and storage facilities. The jetty in *Down by the Jetty* is not the mile-long structure built by Occidental for the delivery of oil across the wide mudflats of Canvey Island before the risk assessment nixed the project, but the album title proleptically invokes the failed and ultimately dismantled Occidental plant the jetty was built to serve and which remains as the last vestige of the enterprise. Shrunk to British proportions, Canvey Island is Detroit-on-sea, another node in the global oil industry where capital flows periodically expand and contract space and determine land use, generate washed-up communities and angry punks among the ruins.

Temple's documentary style borrows liberally from the music promo genre and the interview sections are intercut with found

LANDSCAPE AS WEAPON

footage, movie clips and live performance. Temple projects old footage onto the buildings themselves, a technique borrowed from artists like Horst Hoheisel, who in 1997 projected a photograph of the gates of Auschwitz onto the Brandenburg Gate in Berlin. The effect of this device in *Oil City Confidential* is not exactly subtle but it is arresting and gets closest to the noir sensibility Temple is after in the film. The images are often fleeting and hard to read, but the superimposition of lost worlds of labour, politics and culture upon the very buildings produced out of those worlds articulates a kind of haunted absent presence in these places and also makes literal the fact that the ruin is the site of projection, of imagined pasts not unproblematically authenticated by the physical fact of the building.

The force of the cultural reimagining that underpins the Dr Feelgood narrative – how an impoverished Essex edgeland can spawn strange hybrid creatures and alternative histories – is also there in another project parasitic on the punk imaginary, Laura Oldfield Ford's psychogeographic zinework, *Savage Messiah*.[33] Self-published between 2005 and 2009, and republished in book form in 2011, *Savage Messiah* broadly follows the format of early generations of self-published subcultural art and text – typed out paragraphs pasted over black and white photographs of high rises and back alleys, ballpoint-pen portraits of youth and police, scratchy hand-lettered titles, found scraps of printed matter. Each issue of *Savage Messiah* documents an urban *dérive* around a rundown part of contemporary London. The effect is disorienting, since the local detail is resolutely twenty-first century – gentrification, dispossession, antisocial behaviour, photos of the artist and her friends – but the image repertoire is stubbornly old school, all punk rockers and skinheads, some clearly copied from old magazines and book covers. What is most confusing is not so much the temporal folding of the late 1970s into the early twenty-first century, but the degree to which the form and the format (the original bulletins were pavement-grey Photostats) are reflexively put to work to any critical purpose. Is this, in other words, the authentic product of a 1970s-obsessed Ballardian determined to conjure out of the neo-liberal junkyard a dead-on simulation of a lost world of radical street culture? Or is it a deliberately mannered (Oldfield Ford is a graduate of the Slade and the Royal College of Art), faux primitive retelling of all the cool stuff from that period, from brutalism through Debord and New English Library skinhead novels, photo-romance strips and Crass albums? Is it the real thing? What does this actually mean?

The question of authenticity is especially knotted when it comes to punk rock, which followed the classic subcultural tendency to be at once both insistently Stalinist about origins and intentions (I was a punk before you were a punk) and also smart and ironic in terms of repurposing signs of authenticity from elsewhere (rock 'n' roll accoutrements, dodgy militaria). In Oldfield Ford, this doubleness captures the seemingly irresolvable tension produced by a culture in love with but unable to escape from its past. Drawings appear to come from the observations of an untutored hand wielding a biro. Are these supposed to be the obsessive scribblings of a fictional character, like those psychos in Hollywood films who are always revealed to have filled every inch of their notebooks with dense cod philosophical gibberish? Or is there a genuine bid for expression here, beyond the mannerisms of the punk publication?

Engines Stop Running and the Wheat is Going Thin

On 16 July 2012 the BBC decided not to screen Temple's latest documentary, *London – The Modern Babylon*, which had been scheduled as part of a season of films about the capital in the run-up to the Olympic Games. The film, pieced together from footage from the British Film Institute archives, is an attempt to articulate a century of London life up to and including the 2011 riots. One scene culled from the British gangster film *The Long Good Friday* (1980) imagines a UK Olympic bid for the derelict Docklands area. Whether the BBC decided that images of looting and street-fighting were not the best way to represent London days before the Olympic torch reached the city is unclear, though the broadcaster might have blanched after British Airways thought using The Clash's *London Calling* for the soundtrack to an upbeat Olympic-themed TV commercial was a good idea: ice age, heat death, famine, nuclear error, zombies of death. Here the apocalyptic punk imaginary returns to haunt an affirmative display of corporate engineering designed, presumably, to celebrate British efficiency and London as a global destination. The sheer wrongness of the soundtrack in the British Airways ad is a thrilling act of self-immolation at least as pointed as anything Temple has assembled and also opens up a dream-space where punk nostalgia refuses to capitulate to the restorative logic of the heritage sector and insinuates itself instead into the marketing DNA of the corporation as a mode of auto-*détournement*.

The apocalyptic dimension to the London Olympics is never far away in Iain Sinclair's scrutiny of the destruction of the East End, where the Games are identified as the cataclysmic third act in the dismantling of old London. Sinclair tracked this process from the imagineering of Canary Wharf (*Downriver*, 1991), through the shambles of the Millennium Dome (*Sorry Meniscus,* 1999), and up to the Olympics ('The Olympics Scam', 2008; *Ghost Milk,* 2011). In *Swandown* (2012) Sinclair accompanies film-maker Andrew Kötting on a water-bound journey from Hastings beach to Hackney in a swan-shaped pedalo, a faintly ludicrous riposte to the corporate spectacle of the Olympic circus.[34] On the website for the film, Kötting cites a range of odd southeast coastal precedents for the paddle-boat trip, including Jean-Luc Godard's climax to the Rolling Stones film *Sympathy for the Devil*, filmed at Camber Sands, Scottish artists the Boyle Family's re-creation of randomly chosen areas of the surface of the Earth at Dungeness, and other writers and artists from Henry James and Joseph Conrad to Derek Jarman and Spike Milligan. The pull of the city from the eccentricities of the coast is enacted in *Swandown* as a journey back through the remains of a lost past, the trip punctuated with archival footage and readings from, among others, Edmund Spenser, Edith Sitwell, Conrad, James, Pound, Eliot, Brecht and Werner Herzog.

The avalanche of prior representations that, to a large extent, provides the content for so many contemporary negotiations of ruined or 'regenerated' places – the retinal overload of ruin porn – suggests a culture increasingly built out of its ruins, the endless mash-ups and mutations of sound and vision leading no closer to a retrieval of what has been lost but providing what means there are for a reactivation of energies. In the most successful engagements with this history of ruination, such as Temple's montage strategies, the artists are explicitly self-aware, including shots of themselves working with the archival material or, in *Swandown*, struggling to position the boom mic to record chance meetings. There is little mistaking the fact that the works are the result of ragpicking expeditions in search of revealing juxtapositions, but the reflexivity does signal a critical aperture through which it is made clear that the past is being put to work and not merely the mute object of a devastating homesickness.

3

The Poverty of Ruins

One of the more compelling aspects of John Hillcoat's 2009 adaptation of Cormac McCarthy's novel *The Road* is the fact that the film's post-apocalyptic landscapes are not computer generated but shot on real locations in the United States. Abandoned freeways and strip mines in Pennsylvania, wrecked post-Katrina shopping malls and clouds borrowed from 9/11 footage provide the sources for a space of fictional devastation that remains wedded to the real world. In an era when the indexical function of photography has largely been overruled by computer-generated imagery, the decision to shoot the film in real places creates a kind of reverse-uncanny whereby that which is supposed to be fake is in fact actually there. Hillcoat's aim is, in part, to remind viewers of what they may have already seen rather than to create an unfamiliar nightmare. As he explains, 'the scenes – the forgotten 18-wheeler jackknifed on a freeway bridge, the gas stations littered with useless contraptions, the sinister farmhouses, the sheds with their hand tools piled like ancient contrivances – all of it calls up the now.' It is a world, he insists, that is 'sickeningly familiar'.[1] Part of what is disturbing about Hillcoat's explanation is not just that he is able to find material devastation across the United States, but that such abandonment and redundancy is so commonplace.

To see in the forgotten, the useless and the outmoded evidence of 'the now' is to acknowledge, it seems, a present that is bereft of any obvious purpose and disconnected from history.

It may be true that urban blight and environmental catastrophe are proximate enough that it is not necessary to make them up, but it is also fair to say that the majority of *The Road*'s audience is probably aware of devastation and dereliction largely through their mediation in photography and film. Extreme poverty and despoliation are both close at hand and far away in so-called developed countries, present largely as images of realities held at bay by structural inequality and diligent policing. From the tinted window of the SUV it may be possible to glimpse social collapse on the drive between home and the mall, but this reality is assuredly kept at a safe distance, for the time being, by the place-holding technologies of the property-owning classes. In many ways, the fears *The Road* plays upon are less the terrors of global environmental collapse – though these are real enough – and more related to the horrors of homelessness and destitution caused by radically unstable economic conditions. Being left literally on the road and on foot in the neighbourhood, rather than cruising through it, is perhaps what is really frightening for middle-class moviegoers. Though McCarthy's book was published in 2006, the film entered the public domain in the wake of the U.S. housing crisis and the collapse of Lehman Brothers (the largest bankruptcy in American history), and in the middle of the most devastating economic crisis since the Great Depression. The 2001 terrorist atrocities, the wars in Iraq and Afghanistan, and Hurricane Katrina may have been on McCarthy's mind as he wrote *The Road*, but Hillcoat's treatment is coloured more darkly still by the recession.

The recent preoccupation with ruined and abandoned spaces did not begin with the global economic crisis, but the recession nonetheless accelerated and provided context for a surge of *Ruinenlust* that arose towards the end of the decade and that increasingly came to look like a response to the crisis of capitalism. As the recession deepened so, too, did the fascination with ruination among industrial archaeologists, cultural geographers, philosophers, historians, film-makers, photographers, curators and journalists. While a fascination with industrial infrastructure had previously, if often inadvertently, helped sell boom-time developments that retooled factories and warehouses for 'luxury living', now such projects were left, at least temporarily, unsold, unfinished or forgotten.

Instead, volumes of photographs and streams of documentaries depicted decayed and abandoned cities, and expeditions of urban explorers lit out for the remains of tunnels, bunkers, insane asylums and other decrepit but not yet demolished relics of modernity.[2] These sites are not, by and large, ruins in the sense of being time-softened spaces of forgotten triumphs. Instead, modern dereliction is an accelerated ruin, often created instantly by rapid disinvestment and plant relocation, by freak natural events too costly to clean up, or by a general lack of will, funds or both on the part of city officials and businesses. Mostly, such sites are the rubble left by an economic system in a permanent state of radical transformation, yet the capacity of rubble to be reactivated as ruin, with all the affective and symbolic capital that word delivers, is indicative of a culture in search of a vocabulary with which to account for an inaccessible recent past and a seemingly stagnant and rotting future.[3]

The United States has historically given short shrift to ruins, more often designating the remains, for example, of the ancient cultures of the Americas as mere evidence of dead civilizations or those about to expire, with little to offer the future-oriented

American present. But if the European tradition of ruin gazing as a means of dealing with the depth of time and of reconciling nature and culture has not had much appeal in the U.S., the notion of the ruins of modernity has recently had considerably more leverage in the American cultural imagination.[4] At the same time, in Europe, as we have seen, the growth of interest in cultural memory and the physical and psychological remains of the twentieth century have made the persistence of devastation a major preoccupation. The ruin, in short, has become a signifier of material, social and psychological collapse and the point of convergence through which all manner of losses, failures and crimes can be channelled and embodied.[5] This has been the case whether the context is the belated acknowledgement of ignored or repressed collective memory and traumatic history; an interrogation of the urban devastation of the Second World War; a post-Cold War examination of the previously secret spaces of national security; the heritage industry's capacity to reimagine derelict structures as tourist destinations; pre-recession capitalism's reconstruction of the Fordist workplace as the site for property speculation; the bulldozing of neighbourhoods to produce global financial hubs in cities such as Shanghai and Beijing; or a general desire to seek out the 'authentic' spaces of the past. Not only have the ruins of the twentieth century become the obsession of the twenty-first, but alongside the collections, exhibitions and documentaries dealing with specific cities, regions and nations in dereliction, the climate emergency has introduced the threat of mass extinction, already vividly imagined in *The Road*, as the global fate awaiting a ruined earth.[6]

By turning rubble into ruins, the material evidence of catastrophe has been given aesthetic resonance in a culture struggling to register the speed with which certainties can be detonated and in which centres of power, as well as ways of life, can become dead zones. The vocabulary of 'drosscapes', 'terrain vague' and 'edgelands' has sought to give conceptual shape to post-industrial and other abandoned spaces, but the word 'ruin' remains the most provocative, since it calls forth a history of aesthetic contemplation even as the possibility for the recuperation of economic vandalism and neglect as art must be understood as, at best, problematic and at worst a mode of reactionary political violence. It is this ambivalence at the heart of the term 'ruin' – freighted with picturesque promise but also outrage, and positioned as space and object of undisturbed contemplation but also the very site of disturbance – that allows it to reverberate in so many contemporary contexts.

Inevitably, overexposure to images of modern ruins soon led to complaints of 'ruin porn' as the torrent of dereliction surged forth; even 'ruin porn' itself became a critical cliché.[7] The radical decontextualization that comes with saturation coverage, so much a part of the contemporary media landscape, is especially striking in relation to visualizations of material collapse, since it manages, as it does in films like *The Road*, to fold specific events, processes and locations – deindustrialization, pollution, structural poverty, 9/11, Katrina – into a general, dehistoricized and atemporal representation of disaster. This kind of category slippage allows for a generalized pornification of the discourse surrounding ruination, resulting in the neutralization of historical understanding, fatigue and indifference.

Such an effect, however, is not new. Discussing the politics of urban blight in interwar England and Wales, Denis Linehan claims that in the 'immediate aftermath of World War I, the condition of derelict landscapes and the people within them became part of a wider discourse of postwar crisis which was permeated with fears of civilisational collapse'.[8] The crisis, according to Linehan, was depicted in a 'highly spatialized' manner that was 'directly implicated in tangible issues concerning the condition of people, economies and places'. At the same time, such a reading also 'encouraged the superimposition of physical and psychological space, a factor which was heavily implicated in meanings associated with economic "depression"'.[9] The portrayal of the derelict industrial landscape, Linehan claims, 'often adopted the imagery of the Great War', industrial sites reminding commentators of the battlefields of France and the urban poor situated as 'broken, displaced and defeated'.[10]

At least since the end of the Cold War, and certainly since 9/11 and the growing awareness of the climate crisis, an atmosphere of apprehension and generic 'depression', not unlike Linehan's account of the post-First World War era, has characterized a good deal of cultural life in the U.S. and Europe, where ruins of all kinds have come to embody disquiet and vulnerability. The embrace of the modern ruin might well be a mode of acquiescent and aestheticized submission in the face of an apparently achieved disaster, but the more reflective, contemplative mode of attention historically associated with ruin fascination may not so easily have been snuffed out by the avalanche of ruin porn. The aesthetic legacy of viewing ruins might still provide leverage for a critical interrogation of the relationship between agency (however absent or absconded) and evidence (the material remains). As Christopher Woodward has argued, the ruin is a 'dialogue between an incomplete reality and the imagination of the spectator'.[11] The crucial terms here are 'incomplete' – not only fragmented but unfinished and historically active – and 'imagination'. The imagination's capacity to act upon a derelict building as an incomplete reality suggests an interpretive process that is capable of animating the ruin in ways that push beyond the articulation of defeat. Indeed, to see evidence of war, poverty and natural disaster embodied in ruins is not necessarily a failure to historicize; it can also be a way of making connections between ostensibly unrelated events, providing a critical purchase on otherwise disembodied, mystified causes. As geographer Tim Edensor explains, the production of ruins may be the 'inevitable result' of profit-driven enterprise, but it can also offer space for cultural work where the 'imprint of power on the city' can be challenged and reconfigured.[12]

An Urban Monument Valley

In 1995 photographer and sociologist Camilo José Vergara proposed that twelve square blocks of downtown Detroit be declared a 'skyscraper ruins park', an 'American acropolis' for the preservation and study of deteriorating and empty skyscrapers: this would be a 'grand national historic park of play and wonder, an urban Monument Valley'.[13] Vergara has been reporting on what he calls the 'nature reserve' of the American ghetto for thirty years and his work has been perhaps the single biggest influence on the recent wave of American ruin gazers. While Vergara has recorded derelict neighbourhoods in Harlem, Baltimore, Newark, Chicago and elsewhere, it is Detroit that he nominated as the site of an American acropolis.[14]

Detroit is the only American city to have been regularly described explicitly in the media as a 'ruin' and probably the only one that has, at times, marketed itself accordingly. The paradigmatic rust belt city, Detroit has also become noteworthy in recent years because of its murder rate and because it is shrinking: the population of Detroit has been falling since a 1950 peak of

Camilo José Vergara, Edmunds Place, Detroit, 1998.

1.86 million. In 2000 the population was 951,270; the 2013 U.S. Census recorded 688,701 residents. Five years later, the estimated population stood at 672,662.[15] Although the decline may be slowing, with an average drop of 7,500 a year since 2010, during the 2000s 24,000 residents per year left Detroit.[16] In 2010, according to figures from the Bureau of Labor Statistics for unemployment rates in the fifty largest cities in the U.S., Detroit topped the list with 23 per cent of the city's labour force out of work.[17] The city of Detroit filed for bankruptcy in July 2013, with debts estimated at $18–$20 billion.

Despite its recent notoriety as the epicentre of capitalism's crisis zone, however, the fact is, as the city's shrinking population shows, Detroit has been in decline for a long time – the ruined Detroit buildings in Vergara's work have, in many cases, been abandoned for decades. As the historian Thomas Sugrue explains, the deindustrialization of Detroit began after the Second World

War and accelerated through the 1950s. The story is the now familiar one of plant relocation to cheaper areas with non-unionized labour and white flight. The auto industry led the way in corporate decentralization (some companies relocating to rural areas as early as the 1930s) and in automation. Businesses closed and property values fell; between 1949 and 1960, Detroit suffered four major recessions and thousands of manufacturing jobs were lost, leaving nearly 10 million square feet of idle factory space by 1957.[18] The discourse of growth and affluence during the 1950s marginalized Detroit's economic troubles, according to Sugrue, the collapse of urban economies concealed by national-level statistics.[19] Recent fascination with Detroit's ruins, then, may be driven by recession-era concerns, but the dereliction represents a kind of shadow kingdom of structural abandonment that has deeper roots in capitalism's indifference to the other side of post-war prosperity. It would be a mistake, then, to see the exploration of urban decay in cities like Detroit as merely driven by conservative nostalgia for the industrial prosperity of the 1950s. Certainly, one characteristic of the rise of right-wing populism over the last decade, in the U.S. and elsewhere, has been its willingness to exploit a caricature of post-war social and economic life as the virtuous lost world of security and prosperity destroyed by liberals. A critical examination of the so-called ruins of Detroit, however, demands a more complex understanding of the forces that move through the landscape.

The challenge to that understanding comes, here, in the shredding of contemplation by the pornification of images. At this point, the seemingly trivial complaint about how photography of old wrecked buildings becomes an instant cliché in the modern world starts to look like a symptom of a broader assault on modes of critical attention. Vergara's work, alongside that of Canadian artist Stan Douglas, who exhibited a series of Detroit photographs in 1998, to a large extent established the template for much of the subsequent photographic work on the city's ruins, but in doing so they also inadvertently provided a model for much of the ruin porn to follow. It is hard now, given the proliferation of images, though perhaps not impossible, to register the power of Douglas's image of the astonishing French Renaissance-style ceiling of the huge former Michigan Theater, now used as an ornate canopy for the 160-space car park into which the building has been converted. It is equally difficult to grasp the fearsome singularity of the long-derelict Michigan Central Station, just southwest of downtown, and perhaps the most famous Detroit ruin. It is not inconceivable, perhaps, that when the building was finally sold to Ford in May 2018, to be at the centre of the company's technology campus, part of the attraction was that the building was now, globally, visually familiar as a famous Motor City ruin. The heritage cachet should never be underestimated.

This is not to argue that there is something sacrosanct in abandonment and that nothing should ever be redeveloped. But what is disturbing, and what is enabled by the flattening of criticality by the sludge of over-exposure, is that the kinds of critical project undertaken by photographers like Vergara and Douglas, as well as by sociologist film-makers like George Steinmetz and Michael Chanan, who made a much-copied 2005 documentary, *Detroit: Ruin of a City*, are effectively scrubbed out as the erasing torrent moves through the culture.

The flood of Detroit-based ruin culture that broke through in the wake of the recession and the mortgage crisis turned Detroit into shorthand for all sorts of year-zero narratives, apocalyptic not only in their framing of material devastation but in the often redemptive turn the story arc was encouraged to make, as

Stan Douglas, *Michigan Theatre*, 1997/8, C-print.

film-makers and journalists moved from urban poverty to urban farming, and from structural racism to entrepreneurial art and crafts activism. Three heavyweight books devoted to photographs of Detroit ruins appeared in 2010 alone.[20] Magazines, newspapers and websites across the u.s. and Europe ran heavily illustrated stories.[21] A satirical graphic novel, *Sword of My Mouth* (2010), imagined survivors living in a depopulated Detroit once the Rapture has swept up the righteous. Lowell Boileau's extensive and long-standing, pre-ruin-porn website on the city's decaying architecture, titled 'The Fabulous Ruins of Detroit', served as a reference guide and partly inspired the Steinmetz and Chanan documentary, whose so-called 'drive-by' approach (filming and interviewing from the car) to urban film-making was borrowed by, among others, Briton Julien Temple in *Requiem for Detroit?*

(2010) and *Jackass* star Johnny Knoxville's *Detroit Lives* (2010), a film that combines ruin porn with youth culture boosterism and is sponsored by the Palladium boot company. Film archivist Rick Prelinger produced a found footage documentary called *Lost Landscapes of Detroit* (2010), and French film-maker Florent Tillon's *Detroit Wild City* (2010) foregrounds the entrepreneurs, artists and urban farmers working among the ruins. A further wave of films, including *Deforce* (2010), *Burn* (2012) and *Detropia* (2012), attempted to wrest the history of Detroit back from outside observers and tell the story from the inside.

By 2012 the volume of visual information produced on Detroit had become the story, as indicated by events like that year's 'Imaging Detroit', 48 hours of screenings and performance hosted in the city by the self-described 'nomadic research organization', the Metropolitan Observatory for Digital Cultural and Representation (MODCaR), which sought to curate the torrent while, inevitably, generating more.[22] For MODCaR Detroit is 'a symbolic test site for the reconfiguration of the collective urban experience'. Arguing that 'urban experience is conditioned by images', MODCaR Detroit aimed to show how 'the cumulative image precedes the city, conditions our very perception of it, and suggests that the self-reflexive embrace of this effect may have transformative potential'.[23] This is ruin porn turned against itself, with excessive exposure to images of Detroit conceived as a constitutive environment for critical interrogation rather than an anaesthetizing spectacle. What MODCaR recognized is that, as Detroit-based poet and academic Barrett Watten notes, 'a political use of documentary evidence over the past decade has raised the level of visual literacy on urbanism and Detroit and created a strong relationship between representation and activism.' For Watten, challenging the 'false positivism' of 'illusions of progress and hope' is the 'first task of ruin photography'.[24] Here, images of social negativity are seen not as contributing to narratives of decline but as still capable of opening up vital critical spaces.

What Watten sees as a critical opportunity made possible through politically motivated documentary, others view more sceptically as a misrepresentation of the realities of urban living in Detroit and as a mode of visual appropriation and exploitation. The idea of 'Detroit' here, as a signifier of photogenic urban desolation, threatens to cut loose from any attachment to a real place and circulate, in endless modifications, in ways no longer responsible to any recognizable lived reality. The first option here (ruin photographs as a critical space) is not necessarily cancelled by the fact of the second (ruin photos as ruin porn), though the space available for criticality within the blizzard of twenty-first-century meme culture is not generous or very durable. What MODCaR and Watten both identify, though, is the power of the image as a force that is not separate from, but bound up with, the production of the meaning of the city. As such, even in its degraded and viral forms, the ruin photograph participates in an ongoing argument concerning the contested identity of what Detroit was and remains.

Struggles over the representation of the city have long been at the heart of Detroit-based urban investigations. The power of an incisive visualization is nowhere more apparent than in geographer William Bunge's cartographic interventions in the late 1960s. Bunge, based then at Wayne State University, and Gwendolyn Warren, an eighteen-year-old African American community organizer, led the short-lived but influential Detroit Geographical Expedition and Institute (DGEI). Formed shortly after the 1967 riots in the city, the Expedition intended to bring together academic geographers and what Bunge called 'folk' geographers (local people) in order to map the city as it was and as it ought to be. The Institute ran an educational programme whereby Detroit residents could take free classes for college credits offered through the University of Michigan (1969) and then Michigan State University (1970). Faculty worked on a volunteer basis. Yearly expeditions in Detroit investigated a pressing social problem, enlisting residents to participate in the production of knowledge. The results of the expeditions were compiled annually between 1969 and 1972 in 'Field Notes'. Bunge published his account of his own Detroit neighbourhood, *Fitzgerald: Geography of a Revolution*, in 1971. The expedition mapped the distribution of taverns and bars and children's playing fields in a neighbourhood (there were many more bars), the number of rat-bitten babies in the part of the city most prone to sightings of rats, and charted the sites, as the title of the map explains, 'Where Commuters Run Over Black Children on the Pointes-Downtown Track'.

The activist spirit of the DGEI never really left Detroit and it is there, I think, in Vergara's insistence that the 'ruins' of the city speak not only to the history of racism and disinvestment, but to the capacity to reimagine the city beyond the capitalist model of endless growth.[25] Bunge's example also shines through in architect Andrew Herscher's Detroit Unreal Estate Agency, an open-access platform for the study of urban crisis focused on the city. In his *The Unreal Estate Guide to Detroit* (2012), Herscher catalogues a huge range of architectural initiatives, art projects and community activities that variously reimagine what a city might be.[26] At the same time, accounts by so-called urban pioneers, such as Drew Philp's narrative of his adventure renovating a Detroit house he purchased for $500, have contributed to an upbeat version of Detroit as the laboratory of some kind of emancipatory post-capitalist survivalism.[27] Bunge was aware, in his use of a term like

LANDSCAPE AS WEAPON

Expedition, of the colonialist legacies he had dragged into view, and in *Fitzgerald*, his own struggles with the burden of his white middle-class background are clear. Philp, likewise, though he stresses his family's blue-collar origins, also recognizes that his project is plausible in large part because of his race and education (in his apartment block, at work and at the bar, he is often the only white face). For all their defiant enterprise and activist spirit, the kind of projects outlined by Herscher and others seem like compensations rather than solutions to structural inequality and abandonment. Their experimental nature is exciting and inventive, but it is hard to shake the suspicion that the art projects and community neighbourhood reclamations function mainly as a prelude to some form of gentrification.

Part of the problem remains the way representations of derelict Detroit were too easily repurposed as generic apocalyptic images of capitalism in crisis during the recession. What images from the 1990s like those by Douglas and Vergara reveal is a deeper urban crisis that is less about capitalism failing and more about capitalism as a successful and self-sustaining engine of inequality. What Douglas's and Vergara's images depict is not a collapsed economy at all, but a radically redistributed population along lines of class and race. The American automobile industry remains headquartered in Detroit regardless of how many derelict factories there are, and while the city of Detroit is profoundly impoverished, as Rebecca Kinney argues, the metropolitan region is among the nation's most prosperous.[28] What Vergara's images of a depopulated Detroit effectively deliver, according to Kinney, is evidence that the once all too visible black bodies of the 'urban ghetto' – overcrowded, poor, prone to rioting – have been made to disappear. This shift, explains Kinney, 'from representing Detroit as a site of urban nightmare to a nearly empty city reconverting to pastoral landscape lays the visual foundation of Detroit as fertile ground, a concept that will be embraced full scale in the narratives of redevelopment that emerge in the 2000s'.[29] It is hard not to conclude from Kinney's remarks that ruin porn played an important part in laying this foundation, not merely by decontextualizing the complex economic and social history represented by the derelict buildings, but by shaping the image of the post-apocalyptic city as an available space for creative refashioning.

Drive-by Shooting

As I have suggested, the pre-recession work on Detroit may have established the terms adopted by ruin porn, but it was often, as in Vergara and Douglas, underpinned by a deeper sense of investigative commitment. This is true of Steinmetz and Chanan's *Detroit: Ruin of a City* (2005), which stylistically set the tone for Detroit documentaries through its combination of archive footage and mobile interviews, but is also the most self-aware in terms of the possibilities and limitations of critique. The extensive use of archive film not only reinforces the gap between what contemporary Detroit has become and what it was, but, as Chanan explains, reveals how the history of the city is 'a battle of representation which began when Ford instructed his advertising department to start making films before the U.S. entered the First World War'.[30] Here, in anticipation of the contested representation of the city produced by the torrent of ruin porn, Steinmetz and Chanan see the struggle between the official version and critical interrogations of urban history as formal as well as interpretive, and the challenge they face is to produce a record of decay that does not reproduce a kind of inverted boosterism that replays dereliction as aesthetic recuperation, a charge sometimes made against Vergara's work.[31]

Steinmetz and Chanan recognize the problem and explain that they 'try to steer a course' between the 'seduction of Ruinenlust' and 'the widespread pathologisation of the city found in crime reporting and Hollywood's urban dystopias'. At the same time, though, Steinmetz notes that a third danger would be 'to avoid the ruins altogether and to produce a polyannish boosterism that ignores the real problems and raises false hopes'.[32] As a consequence, rather than focusing on depopulated spaces, Steinmetz and Chanan, unlike Vergara and other still photographers, sought out the local population and record their histories. Here, the 'drive-by' approach is positioned as a self-conscious incursion from the outside that does not elide the dangers of ethnographic tourism but, much like Bunge's 'expedition' or Vergara's national park idea, foregrounds and amplifies the move from outside to inside. To a degree, and in coining the 'drive-by' descriptor, Steinmetz and Chanan allow the preconceptions and prejudices of the non-city dweller to be aired and directly interrogated. Nevertheless, a 'drive-by' approach does lean on the term's negative associations with racialized urban crime narratives, and when Steinmetz explains that when they drive into the city, 'rather than being mugged we encounter a population that is extraordinarily eager to talk, to be represented', there is a real danger that the outsider status of the film-makers reproduces the racial and class prejudices their work is determined to challenge.

Despite the risks, though, the reflexivity of Steinmetz and Chanan's approach is intended to establish some distance between observers and subject in order to resist the calculated but intrusive intimacy of the objective gaze in its first-hand report from a strange land. Their outsider status is confronted, claims Steinmetz, 'head on by staging the film as a "road movie" in which we are continually entering the city from the outside, haplessly losing our way, asking naïve questions, learning as we go, and "changing" our view of the city'. By embracing the awkwardness of their ability to navigate the city, the film-makers allow a deflationary irony to prevent the film becoming a bulletin from the warzone or a version of the colonial encounter. As such, *Detroit: Ruin of a City* shares with Robert Smithson, and with Sinclair and Petit in *London Orbital*, a self-awareness that is prepared to risk a perverse and unstable mixture of exploitation and resistance.

Like Smithson, Sinclair and Petit, who read their contemporary landscapes as encoded messages about the deep structures and processes out of which forms emerge, Steinmetz and Chanan see in Detroit's post-industrial ruins not merely evidence of depletion and abandonment, but something deeper, something that speaks to a failure of historical imagination. Unlike sites of 'disgrace and catastrophe' in Europe and elsewhere, Steinmetz complains, 'American ruins have not been recognized by the state or by important sectors of the public as worthy of preservation.' Detroit's ruins, he goes on, 'are not accorded the dignity of official "realms of memory" or *lieux de memoire*' and have been left 'as socially unsignified remnants'. If Steinmetz and Chanan thought their film might begin to remedy that situation, they probably did not expect the hypertrophied, and largely undignified, over-signification of Detroit ruins by ruin pornographers. Even as Steinmetz and Chanan were working to situate parts of Detroit as dignified sites of American disgrace and catastrophe, Hollywood had found a less reflective way of redeeming the ruins.

The Road is about the struggle of an unnamed man to protect his son from the cannibalistic remains of humanity, to train the boy to survive and, as he puts it, 'carry the fire' of decency into an inhospitable future. This concern is shared by Clint Eastwood's *Gran Torino* (2008), where the last man trope is played out in the blighted blue-collar suburbs of contemporary Detroit. In *Gran Torino* the apocalypse is social, Eastwood's Kowalski, an embittered ex-auto worker making a last stand against the gang-ridden streets where he is the only remaining white face. As Kowalski is drawn into the lives of the Hmong family next door, he takes on the job of 'manning up' the teenage Thao who is close to being sucked into the criminal gang culture of his peers. As in *The Road*, the patriarch must die after passing on the 'fire' in order to release the son into a ruined future. In *Gran Torino*, the 'fire' is, of course, a car.

Gran Torino was shot on location in Detroit, around Highland Park, Grosse Pointe Park and other areas; while the original story was set in Minnesota, the economic incentives for filming in Michigan made Detroit financially more attractive, beyond the symbolism of setting a film about an old car in Motor City. In 2008 Michigan decided to offer generous tax incentives to film-makers, with a refundable tax credit of up to 42 per cent for production costs spent in the state. This trumps even Louisiana, which offered up to 35 per cent. From only two films made in Michigan in 2007, the Michigan Film Office claimed that in 2008, 35 films were produced, spending $135 million. The figure rose dramatically again for 2009, with $223 million spent in the state.[33] Around 80 per cent of the productions drawn to Michigan by tax breaks were shot in Detroit, a city ideal for film-makers who, as *USA Today* observed, 'can close off entire blocks for weeks without worrying about disrupting the city's flow'.[34] The *Wall Street Journal* asked bluntly: 'Want to blow up a building, or burn it down? Detroit is happy to help' so long as you pay for the demolition and clean-up yourself.[35] The radically under-populated city makes Detroit, one director noted, 'the definition of a back lot'.[36] Eastwood's Kowalski is the human counterpart of the ruins of Detroit, memorialized but done for and sacrificed in the name of a dubious aesthetic. Yet the short-sightedness of *Gran Torino*'s nostalgia for white male dignity forged through manufacturing means that it is incapable of acknowledging the fact that the film itself can only exist due to the predations of Hollywood and the concessions of local government.

If *Gran Torino* is hardly radical in its depiction of urban decline, it is light years more advanced than its British double, the Michael Caine vehicle *Harry Brown* (2009), which replays the former film's old-tough-decent-guy-teaches-broken-society-a-lesson narrative with the same self-referential chops (this time it is Harry Palmer and Jack Carter instead of Dirty Harry and Josey Wales) and the same collapsed infrastructure. *Harry Brown* was mainly filmed in and around the Heygate and Aylesbury estates near Elephant and Castle, southeast London. The Heygate, completed in 1974, was demolished, despite protests, between 2011 and 2014. The Aylesbury, built between 1963 and 1977 was, like the Heygate, a popular location for scenes of urban dereliction, though it is currently in the middle of a twenty-year, phased demolition and regeneration programme.[37] *Harry Brown* premiered at the Toronto International Film Festival in September 2009; a month later Clint Eastwood was at the Heygate estate on a location shoot for *Hereafter* (2010).

Harry Brown taps into the same vein of conservative vigilante nostalgia as *Gran Torino* and both films are reliant upon the authenticity of the urban milieu that they depict and the cut-price filming this offers. They both imagine contemporary urban space as bereft of purpose and read the majority of the non-geriatric population as irredeemably feral. *Harry Brown*'s villain is played by Ben Drew, the rapper also known as Plan B, who functions as a kind of extradiegetic British Eminem (Marshall Mathers spent his teenage years in Detroit, also the setting for the 2002 film *8 Mile*). Drew cemented his reputation as a voice of the underclass by recording an angry state-of-the-nation album and directing his own urban crime drama set in post-2011 riots London. Both album and film are titled, with suitably lumpen bad-boy irony, *Ill Manors* (2012). The Detroit–East London correspondences, however, are complicated in *Harry Brown* by a particular aesthetic that derives from a European as well as an American lineage.

The cinematographer on *Harry Brown*, Martin Ruhe, also worked on Anton Corbijn's biopic of Joy Division's Ian Curtis, *Control* (2007). It was Corbijn's atmospheric late 1970s black and white photographs of the band that were in large part responsible for the post-industrial visual style of Joy Division: Salford by way of Eastern Europe, high-rise flats and flyovers. Ruhe managed to recreate that look for *Control*, and the same aesthetic is at work in *Harry Brown*. Chris Petit's *Radio On* (1979) achieved a similar crossover by using Wim Wenders's cinematographer, Martin Schaefer, to shoot the London to Bristol run in New German Cinema monochrome. Wenders's own fascination with American film is well known and the transposition of familiar Hollywood genre codes to a European setting characterizes much of his work of the 1970s and 1980s, not least in the road movie trilogy so important to Petit, *Alice in the Cities* (1974), *The Wrong Move* (1975) and *Kings of the Road* (1976), but also in his use of Dennis Hopper in *The American Friend* (1977) and his homage to the Western, the L. M. Kit Carson and Sam Shepard-scripted *Paris, Texas* (1984). What one of the most vivid, if depressing, British urban noirs since the 1970s has achieved, then, is a fusion of indigenous Free Cinema urban grit and Ballard-inflected apocalyptic alienation with Euro-mediated American noir by way of 1970s Hollywood.

The success of the wave of American and British vigilante and alienated authority figure films of the early 1970s, from *Dirty Harry* and *The French Connection* (1971) to *Get Carter* (1971) and *Death Wish* (1974), relied on a combination of post-1968 disenchantment and right-wing backlash, but the broader context is the collapsing infrastructure of the city, from New York City to Newcastle upon Tyne, and the sense of a degraded population under-employed and in thrall to drugs, promiscuity and violent criminality.[38] The nose-diving American and British economies opened up swathes of industrial dereliction and social ruin that was exploited in films that again and again stressed the need for authoritarian retribution and a violent cleansing of the corrosive consequences of post-war progressivism. Retrofitted revenge dramas like *Gran Torino* and *Harry Brown* seem like a return to the early 1970s not just because they resurrect the same actors, but because they are films spawned out of economic recession and the moral panic that is so often the enabling fiction that would blame the poor for the woes of the nation.

The ruined urban landscapes within which these dramas take place are also, however, the enabling spaces within which a counter-narrative of subtopian dereliction continues to challenge the scorched-earth policy of asset strippers and neo-liberal vigilantes. The resurrection of Eastwood and Caine as twenty-first-century retreads of what already looked like suspect moral certainties in the 1970s has been accompanied by a reappraisal of the punk noir of the 1970s as a complex reminder of a future that did not happen: the critical cultural spaces of the pre-Reagan, pre-Thatcher years before high finance retooled Fordist ruins as gentrified gated 'communities'.

The necessary ambivalence in Steinmetz and Chanan's work and in Temple's films – the discomfort as well as the brio with which wrecked places and people are approached – is precisely what is disturbingly absent from major studio releases like *The Road*, *Gran Torino* and *Harry Brown*. These films are unambiguously conservative narratives with a prurient regard for that which they purport to despise, piously offering restorative justice and patriarchal continuity in the face of an achieved or imminent apocalypse that most people, if these stories are to be believed, probably deserve.

In a very real sense, those films, as much as they are throwbacks to a paranoid 1970s vision of white victimization, also vividly anticipate the reactionary politics of the populist Right in post-2016 Europe and the U.S. Among the many post-war white working class wish fulfilment fantasies exploited in *Gran Torino* and *Harry Brown* is the idea of the stubborn old man who refuses to move out. While white flight, as a function of white privilege, allowed blue-collar workers during the 1950s and 1960s to make enough money to 'escape' the 'inner city', as a narrative of victimization this is figured as a necessary retreat from unwelcome interlopers. The Eastwood and Caine figures, in refusing to flee, become heroic not just because they fight back but because their attachment to place overrides their best interests. So in a puzzling but all too familiar sense, they are allowed to be heroes and victims at the same time, racist and non-racist, old-fashioned yet capable of responding to the urgent demands of the present. They did not 'better' themselves by moving to the suburbs but stuck it out because they were there first. What revanchist fantasies like *Gran Torino* and *Harry Brown* neglect to mention, though, is that it is more likely to be the developers, in league with local government and foreign investors, and not immigrants, that finally oust the reactionary old white men from their estates.

Like the Heygate and Aylesbury estates, the celebrated Robin Hood Gardens in Poplar, east London, designed by Alison and Peter Smithson and completed in 1972, is in the process of being demolished. Despite its global reputation as an icon of modern architecture, attempts to preserve the building by securing listed status failed. The site is part of a wider redevelopment project called Blackwall Reach, just as the site of the Heygate and Aylesbury estates are part of the Elephant Park project. The starting price for a two-bedroom flat at Blackwall Reach is around £650,000. Since the financial crisis, as Anna Minton explains, foreign investment has poured millions into the London property market, while councils, struggling with austerity budgets, have been busy striking deals to cross-subsidize social housing by selling off real estate, including old council estates like Robin Hood Gardens, to private developers.[39]

One of the reasons investors want to buy properties in new urban developments is because cities have been refashioned in the last few decades by artists, designers and others capable of perceiving new ways of living in old, unwanted parts of town, or because the people who live in old, unwanted parts of town are capable of living in ways that remain appealing despite their hardships. Here, the ruin narrative and the aesthetic value it bestows upon the neglected and deprived is at once redeeming (it transforms squalor into desire) and catastrophic (once desirable, it becomes profitable). The typical outcome of this process, as Bruce Katz and Jeremy Nowak write in their recent argument for a 'new localism' in urban planning, is 'tenant replacement', as 'yesterday's artists' lofts become tomorrow's investment bankers' condos'.[40] Katz and Nowak, despite their upbeat embrace of private–public partnerships, have disappointingly little to say about this transfer of ownership other than 'issues of affordability have to be addressed'. What is important for us to remember, they write, is that 'many of those buildings were underused or abandoned, and their transformation into active use is a contribution to public and private wealth'.[41]

It is through art that abandonment is recoded as desire; that (mis)perception may also be a form of blindness, misconstruing poverty as 'local colour' or 'emptiness'. When Vergara imagines Detroit as an American Acropolis or as a new urban prairie, he recalls, to my mind, Robert Smithson's notion of Passaic, New Jersey, as the Eternal City. These comparisons are serious, in that they invite critical reflection around issues of cultural value and temporality, but they are also bathetic and playful, reflexively recognizing the tendency of art to radically scramble categories, to turn ephemera and detritus into value. Bunge provocatively rescued the word 'expedition' in the same way that Vergara appropriates the notion of the 'nature reserve' and Steinmetz and Chanan reimagined their documentary as a 'drive-by' road movie – it is a risky ploy, invoking the colonial sensibility in its relation to the other. But it is a provocation with a point, it dares a confrontation and it acknowledges, however uncomfortably, the asymmetries that are built in to any engagement with the city from the outside. These questions of identification and appropriation, of inside and outside, inhabitant and tourist, are not specific to the city, but they burn fiercely there.

The American artist Mike Kelley grew up in a 1950s single-storey ranch-style house in a working-class suburb of Detroit. Before his suicide in January 2012, Kelley had been working on a project called *Mobile Homestead*, involving the construction of a full-size replica of his childhood home to be relocated in the centre of Detroit in a reversal of the white flight of the 1960s and '70s. Kelley drove the shell of the house through the city, from the

Mike Kelley's *Mobile Homestead* in front of Michigan Central Station in Detroit.

Museum of Contemporary Art Detroit (MOCAD) out to his original home in Westlake and back, stopping to interview residents along the way. The mobile home, which opened in 2013, now sits permanently on land adjacent to MOCAD where the first level, accessible to the public, rests atop two maze-like underground floors built into the earth that function as secretive, private spaces. Marsha Miro, president of the board of MOCAD, explained before the opening that 'It's a suburban house put back into the city,' reintroducing 'some of the things that people do in suburbs that have been taken way from people in Detroit, like swings and slides'.[42] Miro is in danger of overselling the project here, I think, since it is not the paraphernalia of a lost suburban utopia that Kelley has restored to the city with the project. Rather, it is the radical disjunction between downtown dereliction and suburban neatness that has been materialized through the introduction of

LANDSCAPE AS WEAPON

one space into the other that gives *Mobile Homestead* its power. Like Kötting and Sinclair's swan boat, the images of a suburban dwelling being freighted through town signal a disquieting mixture of melancholy and camp. There is something funereal about these works, but the gravity is punctured by the excessive non-instrumentality of the act.

The volume of ruin porn photographs of Detroit turned the city into an empty symbol of destructive capitalism but did little to address the causes of urban decay and the poverty and homelessness that accompany it. Berlin-based American artist Bryan Mendoza became a target of criticism when in 2016 he bought a derelict Detroit house and had it dismantled and shipped to Rotterdam where it was rebuilt for an art fair. Mendoza claims that he was unprepared for the political storm he stirred up in Detroit, where the project was interpreted as a predatory move that took advantage of the economic situation in the city. He knew enough, however, to take on another house, presented to him by Rhea McCauley, the niece of Civil Rights hero Rosa Parks, who had bought Parks's old house in Detroit for $500 to save it from demolition. Mendoza packed up the house and reassembled it outside his studio in Berlin. The house was returned to the U.S. in 2018, where it was installed at the WaterFire Arts Center in Providence, Rhode Island, before being auctioned with a minimum bid of $1 million. At the time of writing, negotiations are ongoing among a pair of Detroit businessmen, a university and a foundation. Whoever finally owns the Rosa Parks house, it is unlikely to be destroyed.

The vague boosterism of Miro's account of the Kelley project suggests that *Mobile Homestead* could end up simply adding to the cultural capital of Detroit as America's ruin theme park. There is, in the end, no outside of the ruin, since dereliction is always both evidence of abandonment and an invitation for revenue generation. As Edensor claims, though, the ruin can be an opening, a gap or rupture in the seamless management of urban space by capital. In the interim, in the dead time and dead space between abandonment and reuse, the ruin might allow for challenges to 'the imprint of power on the city'.[43] The ruin is less a site than a threshold and a pause, a holding space where materialized temporalities converge. The message from the past – punk's 'no future' – haunts the ruin, but it is not the foreclosure of linear time that was anticipated in the slogan and instead a denial of linearity itself.

4
___

Invisible from Here On In

In February 2009 the French artist Cyprien Gaillard excavated a
former Nazi communications bunker buried on a hill overlook-
ing the beach in the Duindorp (Dunepark) neighbourhood of
Scheveningen near The Hague. Constructed in 1943 as part of
Hitler's Atlantic Wall, the bunker, like many others, was abandoned after the war, but since demolition was difficult and
expensive this unwelcome reminder of occupation and conflict
was, literally, buried. Working with earth-moving equipment and
local volunteers, Gaillard diligently scooped away the sand and
pressure-washed the exposed structure. Crowds watched the
process and children clambered over the concrete. At the end of
March, Gaillard reburied the bunker.

Nowhere are the themes and concerns addressed in this book
more entwined than in the decommissioned military site. The
pillbox, observation post, command centre and defensive redoubt
combine the isolation of the depopulated rural landscape, the
edgeland meeting of wilderness and infrastructure, and the
awesome materiality of the technological sublime so often
encountered in urban exploration, with the raggedness of
the modern ruin. The military bunker is the site for military-
industrial pastoral melancholy, science-fiction apocalyptic

Cyprien Gaillard's excavated bunker. *Dunepark* (2009), installation with German bunker at Scheveningen, The Hague, Netherlands.

fantasy, Brutalist-inspired concrete reverie, and retro mid-century authoritarian nostalgia. As with the other over-exposed icons of early twenty-first-century landscape, though, it would be unwise to dismiss the fixation on bunkers merely as a version of ruin porn.

The French architect and theorist Paul Virilio describes the Atlantic Wall bunker as a milestone or stele, a monument or commemorative slab that speaks, through its position and configuration of materials, of the world it inadvertently memorializes.[1] It is unintentional memorialization because bunkers like these are not supposed to have remained; indeed, they are not supposed to be seen at all. A ruined bunker is not really a building and is more like a piece of discarded armour. 'The monolith', Virilio notes, 'does not aim to survive down through the centuries; the thickness of its walls translates only the probable power of impact in the instant of assault.' Put simply, the bunker 'appears as a survival machine'.[2] The thing that makes a bunker function properly, though – its capacity to withstand impact – is also the thing that makes it last longer than it is supposed to, extending its existence through to times in which it does not really belong. If the bunker's intended purpose is to be a survival machine, it is also a time machine.

Gaillard's excavation reveals a structure that is known but not seen, then conceals it again. The bunker itself is unmoved and unmovable as the earth around it is repositioned, not exactly a found object but a temporarily exposed one. As a version of the cliché of the creative process whereby the sculptor lifts form from the block of stone, here the form is literally already there – prefabricated – and the form is a block. Projects like Gaillard's make plain an inescapable history that has been only awkwardly and incompletely accepted. The process of disinterring and then covering the bunker again draws the bunker back into historical time but only fleetingly, its ambivalent status as an immovable marker of violent domination intact even as it is reburied. While Gaillard's process of showing and hiding affirms a willingness to confront a violent legacy, it also suggests a certain passivity, a concession to the bunker's concrete permanence – its claim to timelessness. Presumably, blowing the thing up was not an option. Bunkers have become an integral part of the European heritage business, their dark presence normalized within a network of visitor-friendly objects and sites. A slow and painstaking dismantling of Gaillard's bunker by volunteers might have given the project more political bite, but its persistent absent presence perhaps speaks more powerfully to the uncomfortable truth of the bunker's existence than no presence at all.

The Degree of Our Insecurity

Early in W. G. Sebald's novel *Austerlitz* (2002), the architectural historian Jacques Austerlitz surmises that it is 'often our mightiest projects that most obviously betray the degree of our insecurity'.[3] This observation is made during a conversation about the folly of military fortifications that, Austerlitz argues, regardless of their technical sophistication, rarely provide the kind of defensive assurance their design and construction promises. A heavily fortified town draws fire because it is obviously a valuable enemy asset; complex barricades push sensible officers to lead the advance elsewhere; and large defensive systems can take so long to build that they are outmoded before they are finished. The immediate context of Austerlitz's comments is the system of ringed defences around Antwerp, begun in 1859 and periodically modified and extended up until the building of the fortress of Breendonk in

1906. By this time the fortifications were already near-useless in the face of modern weapons and many were destroyed by the German artillery during the First World War. Breendonk became a Nazi prison and transit camp during the Second World War, the incarcerated forced to dig out the fort by hand by removing a huge layer of topsoil and using it to build around it a concealing wall. Deployed as a prison after the war to detain collaborators, Breendonk was designated a National Memorial in 1947.

Prompted by his conversation with Austerlitz, Sebald's narrator visits Breendonk, carrying in his mind an image of 'a star-shaped bastion with walls towering above a precise geometrical ground-plan'.[4] Instead, what he encounters is a 'low-built concrete mass' that is 'hunched and misshapen' like the 'broad back of a monster', a structure 'so far exceeding [his] comprehension' that he is 'unable to connect it with anything shaped by human civilization, or even with the silent relics of our prehistory and early history'.[5] The fort is nothing but a 'monolithic, monstrous incarnation of ugliness and blind violence'.[6] *Austerlitz* is not the first time Sebald has had occasion to describe military structures as deformed monuments to barbarism. In *The Rings of Saturn* (1995), the famous concrete pagodas on the shingle spit at Orford Ness in Suffolk that were once part of a secret military installation seem 'like the remains of our own civilization after its extinction in some future catastrophe'.[7] The concrete bunkers here look 'like the tumuli in which the mighty and powerful were buried in prehistoric times with all their tools and utensils, silver and gold'.[8] Lost in space and time, the narrator is bewildered by the 'enigma' the place represents.

In each of Sebald's descriptions of an encounter with the remains of military constructions their monstrous presence is temporally destabilizing. The buildings either seem to have been thrown to earth from some other place or else the visitor himself has been transported through time to glimpse the ruins of the future. The point of these reflections is not to uncouple fortifications from history, though, but to identify something in bunkers that resists assimilation. For Sebald, the bunker generates its own dehistoricizing effect as a kind of negative monument that commemorates an absence and a forgotten context. In the face of its concrete blankness, pre- and post-historical imaginings fill the space evacuated by the bunker's refusal to yield an account of itself. Sebald's discussion of Breendonk and Orford Ness registers the challenge presented by relics of conflict, the ways in which the past is both confirmed and denied by their obstinate presence, and the unease that such structures can still generate.

The bunker is both anomalous and ubiquitous in contemporary culture, betraying, as Jacques Austerlitz says, 'the degree of our insecurity'. Partly this is because bunkers seem to be necessary, even as the evidence suggests that they are largely useless. The solidity of the reinforced bunker invokes the power of the weapons it is intended to repel and also the folly of any attempt to seek shelter from them. This is perhaps most obvious in the case of the continuing fascination with Hitler's bunker, which has its source not only in the imagined thoroughness with which Nazi space was militarized, but in the fact that it ultimately offered no protection. The satisfaction in knowing that Hitler could not secrete himself from Allied assault gives the lie to the bunker's promise of security, but in doing so inadvertently also calls into question the usefulness of the bunker in the first place. Hitler himself had already demonstrated this by steering his invasion of France around the Maginot Line.

The bunker's redundancy as a mode of defence is seemingly confirmed by the remains of thousands of pillboxes, block-houses,

Ground zero for the English military–industrial picturesque: Orford Ness, Suffolk.

fallout shelters, flak towers, observation posts, gun turrets, command centres and test sites that litter cities, coastlines and landscapes from rural East Anglia to Kinmen Island in the Taiwan Strait. These are perhaps the most extensive ruins of the twentieth century, of ideologies, conflicts and dreams of mastery cast in reinforced concrete. Yet the reassuring pastness of the ruin's conventional aesthetic function is not so easily achieved by the wrecked or abandoned bunker, which continues to shape and structure affective responses to the environment within which it squats. 'It is hard', writes Robert Macfarlane of Orford Ness, to 'not feel its militarising influence upon one's vision. That day, everything I saw seemed bellicose, mechanised. A hare exploded from a shingle divot. Bramble coiled and looped like barbed wire. Geese landed with their undercarriages down. Green and orange lichen camouflaged the concrete of pillboxes.'[9] Military ruins here reorder perception along military lines: the bunker militarizes the natural and naturalizes the military. Unlike the time-softened contours of the romantic ruin, for Macfarlane the abandoned military site continues instead to harden and technologize the surroundings. The past to which the bunker stands as evidence is not over but remains the condition of possibility within which the present must be apprehended.

The technologies of modern warfare have required defensive installations to be, above all else, hidden, and part of what disorients Sebald's narrators and what militarizes Macfarlane's prose is the fact that what ought to be concealed has become visible. Rendering the invisible visible is a sign of breached security, hence the disquiet experienced when the otherwise veiled realm of military occupation is exposed to the field of vision.

While the bunker promises security and control in the form of refuge it is also a sign of the deadly power that requires reinforced shelter; a bunker is both womb- and tomb-like, generating precisely the kind of attraction/repulsion ambivalence Freud discusses in *Totem and Taboo* as the characteristic polarity of modern affective life.[10] For Zygmunt Bauman, ambivalence is the 'acute discomfort' produced by a failure of language's naming function to secure an object or event to a single category. Modernity's pursuit of order has, for Bauman, been a protracted war on ambivalence, yet the classification systems that have sought to reduce chaos by fragmenting and regulating the world have in fact only served to generate more ambivalence. Ambivalence, writes Bauman, 'is *the waste of modernity*' and modernity's 'most genuine worry and concern, since unlike other enemies, defeated or enslaved, it grows in strength with every success of modern powers. It is its own failure that the tidying-up activity construes as ambivalence.'[11]

As a sign of modern industrial warfare, the bunker embodies violence either achieved or promised. But, as we have seen, a visible bunker is to a large extent disarmed, though its military function is overwritten by its uncanny affective power as something hidden that has come to light. The control of the environment the bunker's presence was supposed to ensure – the war machine's capacity to secure and hold territory; to produce order from chaos and thereby reduce ambivalence – is, post-war, apparently no longer relevant. And yet, as Macfarlane suggests, the bunker maintains a hold on its environment that cannot properly return to a state of peace but must forever be informed by its militarized condition. The bunker's capacity to generate discomfort of the kind registered by Sebald and Macfarlane is complicated and troublesome; indeed, as Bauman suggests, any attempt to grasp or secure the bunker's significance is likely to produce more ambivalence and contradiction. The bunker as such is disruptively anomalous and defies categorization and stability of function and significance. Oscillating somewhere between the visible and the invisible, architecture and engineering, ruins and rubble, violence and inertia, the spectacularly symbolic and the blankly dumb, the bunker is the waste of modernity that cannot be tidied away.

In the case of Orford Ness, after existing for the best part of a century as a Ministry of Defence secret, the National Trust established the site as a nature reserve in 1993; visitors are divided between birdwatchers and military installation enthusiasts. According to Christopher Woodward, a conscious decision was made not to demolish the pagodas and other structures on the Ness because the site, it was felt, ought to be left as a palimpsest of twentieth-century history and allowed to poetically erode back into dust. Woodward, like Sebald and Macfarlane, recognizes the odd fusion of the organic and the technological at the site, writing that the 'labs seem half-man, half-Nature'. Unlike Macfarlane, though, Woodward prefers a romantic gloss, reading the bunkers not as phenomenologically contaminated and contaminating, but merely 'as banal as any industrial desolation . . . The Cold War is over.'[12] Woodward is too willing to adopt the language of closure here, and while it could be argued that the National Trust has managed to hold in tension the apparent antinomies of militarized landscape and nature reserve, the site's power cannot be shut down so easily. Even though he quotes Sebald at length, Woodward fails to address the foreboding in Sebald's assessment of the Ness, which, as I have already noted, apprehends, as Sebald writes, 'the remains of our own civilization after its extinction in some future catastrophe'.[13] The Cold War is over, but it is not an ending.

Bunker Style

Second World War bunkers can remain as objects of fascination because, however terrible the conflict they stand for may have been, their anachronistic survival confirms the narrative of victory over tyranny. Cold War-era bunkers, on the other hand, whether large complexes or modest family fallout shelters, have different temporal connotations, though Virilio's point about the basic purpose of the bunker as protection from the instant of assault remains. Cold War bunkers are more about the inside than the outside. While the defensive structures of the Second World War were either dismantled or abandoned and ignored, the installations of the Cold War that replaced them were in large part unseen and unknowable to anyone without security clearance. For this reason, for many years Cold War bunkers could only be imagined, as in the sprawling subterranean command posts of films like *Fail*

LANDSCAPE AS WEAPON

Safe (1964) or *Dr Strangelove* (1964), or rendered in surrogate form by the institutional modernism of post-war brutalism. The immediate legacy of vast wartime bunker-building programmes was rarely acknowledged at the time as an influence on the design and implementation processes of post-war planners and architects, a measure of how thoroughly the bunker's ambivalent status – its absent presence – had become a defining condition of the state of permanent global war.

Paul Virilio began investigating the remains of Hitler's Atlantic Wall fortifications along the French coast in 1958. A seven-year period of exploration and documentation resulted in an exhibition of photographs and texts in Paris in 1975–6. This work was published in an English translation in 1994 under the title *Bunker Archeology*.[14] As well as the now-famous photographs of the bunkers themselves, the book offers a series of historical, architectural and phenomenological ruminations on the structures, along with maps and diagrams providing a typology of the fortifications. The project is at once archaeological and historical in its desire to provide accurate documentation of the bunkers and their significance, and also architectural in its concern to place the buildings within the context of European modernism. There is, in addition, however, a powerful aesthetic dimension to *Bunker Archeology* that suggests something of the work of the influential Düsseldorf-based artists Bernd and Hilla Becher, who began their own typological documentation of industrial structures around the same time that Virilio became interested in the bunkers. The Bechers described their collection of images of water towers, mine heads and gas tanks as taxonomies of 'anonymous sculptures', suggesting, *pace* Duchamp, their status as found objects capable of generating precisely the kind of ambivalence between architecture and engineering captured in Virilio's scrutiny of bunkers. The peculiarities of industrial structures, for the Bechers, 'originate not in spite of, but because of lack of design', and it is this apparent absence of design that enabled military construction to evade acknowledgement from architects even as its forms were being utilized in city centres, new towns and university campuses across Europe and North America.[15]

The exhibition of Virilio's project in the mid-1970s came just after the publication of one of the first attempts to survey the military architecture of the twentieth century, Keith Mallory and Arvid Ottar's *Architecture of Aggression* (1973). The preface to this book explains that the authors originally set out to establish a link between modern architecture and military construction – something Virilio's work also explores – but since they found little significant secondary material on twentieth-century military building their main job became inventorial. One of the reasons why there was no sustained architectural study of military construction before the 1970s is because it was not considered to be architecture at all. Mallory and Ottar quote Michael Waterhouse, the Honorary Secretary of the Royal Institute of British Architects, dismissing military building in 1943 as merely 'a combination of Organisation and Improvisation'. Such buildings 'cannot be called Architecture', sniffed Waterhouse, 'either as we knew it – or as we know it ought to be'.[16] For Waterhouse, the military structure, as an engineering solution to a practical problem, is inconceivable in architectural terms. The military–industrial look of post-war buildings by Le Corbusier, Alison and Peter Smithson and a host of lesser-known city architects such as Birmingham's John Madin was a deliberate challenge to the aesthetic conservatism of establishment figures like Waterhouse, though the purported functionalism of modernist architecture was often an alibi for what was primarily a concern with effect. As Reyner Banham argues, if the 'form follows function' edict had been followed scrupulously 'there would be no way in which a design school could look like a factory'.[17] There may be sound reasons why Madin's Birmingham library, sadly now demolished, was built to resemble a flak tower, but necessity is unlikely to be among them.

If modern architecture was more concerned with style than function, what Virilio's bunker archaeology does is force into view that which is repressed by the utopian futurism of post-war international modernism: that the passive-aggressive look and feel of modernist building projects draw upon the affective and symbolic weight of the military bunker and thereby continue the legacy of militarized space they purport to replace. At the same time, Virilio's attention to exposed structures that should otherwise remain concealed speaks to the impact of a revealed militarized environment that chimes with Macfarlane's experience at Orford Ness. The bunker, writes Virilio,

> is spun from a network under tension with the landscape and, through the landscape, with the region in its expanse. It is an invisible and immaterial network that escapes our gaze and enables the bunker to hide from view and to avoid shocks.[18]

To fulfil its defensive function the bunker must be hidden and naturalized:

> Linked to the ground, to the surrounding earth, the bunker, for camouflage, tends to coalesce with the geological forms whose geometry results from the forces and exterior conditions that for centuries have modeled them.[19]

Once exposed, it is not only the combatant who is vulnerable to the shock of assault but also the viewer who has had the 'invisible and immaterial network' of militarized forces thrust into view.

Virilio's work dissolves the phony distinction between bunkers and modern buildings, a distinction that served as a classificatory containment of the bunker's real and symbolic violence. But while the aestheticized 'architectural' bunker surrogates that became the default style of Cold War state modernism appropriated the effect of the military installation's look of defiance, they also served to deflect the gaze away from the sites of real power, which were anonymously installed elsewhere. As we have seen, effective bunkers are hidden; only redundant bunkers can be seen. An architectural style based on operationally compromised fortifications is patently more interested in form than function, and brutalism's performative machismo works as a mode of camouflage or misdirection since real Cold War architecture, as Tom Vanderbilt has argued, is less about buildings and more concerned with the web of 'security arrangements' that maintained order.[20] Most effective Cold War military buildings were indeed hidden and even those that could be viewed from the outside, like the Pentagon, kept their interiors secret. What was secret, Vanderbilt explains, 'was often right out in the open, and what was "bunkerlike" was often far removed from traditional connotations of defense'.[21]

Virilio's Atlantic Wall explorations are, I think, as much a response to the concealments of Cold War power as they are a historical excavation of the militarization of space during the Second World War. By approaching bunkers as sculptural and architectural forms rather than just as monstrous fascist excrescences, he allows room for the aesthetic within the realm of the barbarous and also brings together wartime engineering with post-war modernism. Interrogating the visibility of 'dead' bunkers and buildings that look like bunkers calls forth an awareness of other unseen bunkers that are in use, the dead bunkers gesturing towards unknown 'live' continuations of their legacy.[22] Virilio argues that the

> bunker has become a myth, present and absent at the same time: present as an object of disgust instead of a transparent and open civilian architecture, absent insofar as the essence of the new fortress is elsewhere, underfoot, invisible from here on in.[23]

A wrecked bunker is never safe since its very presence speaks to the continuation of its power elsewhere.

If the bunker's ambivalence has made its status as architecture a matter of dispute, the aesthetic awkwardness of military structures is also a challenge when considering the bunker as ruin. For Paul Hirst, the particularity of the ruin aesthetic does not apply to bunkers, which are neither heroic nor ancient and as such cannot properly be described as picturesque. While they may well be in a state of advanced disrepair, the aesthetic features of bunkers are, for Hirst, '*sui generis*, a function of their form and site, and those are not altered by the fact the building is no longer in use'.[24] As a block of concrete, disuse or damage does not change the basic form of a bunker; instead, it is often, as we have seen, its incongruous presence in a landscape that makes the bunker remarkable.

Growing interest in the wreckage and remains of war has led to a significant modification of the definition of what constitutes a ruin. While concurring with Hirst that bombs produce rubble and not ruins, in recent years, Andreas Huyssen has observed, the market has 'been saturated with stunning picture books and films . . . of the ruins of World War II. In them, rubble is indeed transformed, even aestheticized, into ruin.'[25] Huyssen is not specifically referring to bunkers, but this aesthetic transformation of rubble into ruins provides a vocabulary for addressing recent conflict that has become central to the exploration of the bunker's cultural significance. One of the dangers here is that the recuperation of bunkers as ruins produces a form of what Brian Dillon calls a 'military-industrial sublime' that risks degenerating into nostalgia.[26]

In a culture unable or unwilling, as we have seen throughout this book, to give up even the more devastated remains of the recent past, the charge of nostalgia is a complicated but common one. The cautious exploration of repressed or traumatic histories in recent decades, and especially since the end of the Cold War, has also been accompanied by an accelerated commodification of all aspects of the past in its material and symbolic forms. Nostalgia is often the name given to a kind of bad-faith version of history and serves as shorthand for what is taken to be a reified, simplified or sentimentalized reduction of complex sites, events and experiences. Although the pull of nostalgia is in some ways integral to the bunker's ambivalent status as modern ruin, it might, to some extent, be arrested or repositioned by deploying a distinction made by Svetlana Boym between what she calls 'restorative' and 'reflective' nostalgia. For Boym, restorative nostalgia is about 'patching up the memory gaps' and rebuilding a much longed for but lost home.[27] As such, restorative nostalgia is ultimately reactionary and typically found in nationalist movements invested in recreating notionally lost traditions, values and institutions. Reflective nostalgia, on the other hand, is about the 'imperfect process of remembrance'; it is not about returning to the past but about understanding 'the irrevocability of the past' through

LANDSCAPE AS WEAPON

'shattered fragments of memory and temporalize[d] space'.[28] Reflective nostalgia is, in short, ambivalent.

Huyssen sees the fascination with industrial and military 'ruins' as part of a broader obsession with 'urban preservation, remakes, and retrofashions, all of which seem to express a fear or denial of the ruination by time'.[29] Hirst's objection to the bunker-as-ruin is correct if the conventions of the picturesque still hold, but for Huyssen, the 'chance for things to age and become ruin has diminished in the age of turbo capitalism'. Instead of the time-softened relics of previous ages, the twenty-first-century ruin is, Huyssen argues, 'either detritus or restored age'.[30] This assessment captures something of the peculiarities of the bunker's contemporary relevance. The awkwardness of the bunker's status within conventional categories of monument, architecture and ruin, precisely because of the bunker's ambivalent place in the cultural imaginary, reveals how bunkers have come to embody intensely and necessarily conflicted attitudes towards power, security and history.

The bunker in many ways functions in contemporary culture as a site of trauma, which, as Cathy Caruth explains, produces an 'oscillation between a *crisis of death* and the correlative *crisis of life*: between the story of the unbearable nature of an event and the story of the unbearable nature of its survival'.[31] Bauman's notion of ambivalence is predicated on the fact of modernity's generation of permanent crisis, and Caruth's conception of history as an oscillation between forms of unbearability is one form that this crisis might take.

Open Secrets

Bunkers around the world have become ready-made tourist attractions since the end of the Cold War. Mallory and Ottar's complaint in the early 1970s that there was little published on military construction has been answered by an avalanche of illustrated guides, handbooks and websites. The Defence of Britain Project, for example, funded by the Heritage Lottery Fund and the Imperial War Museum and run by the Council for British Archaeology between April 1995 and December 2001, employed six hundred volunteers to record nearly 20,000 twentieth-century anti-invasion defence sites across the UK. The project's findings produced two huge online databases and a growing library of publications.[32] Specialist publishers such as Osprey offer a series looking at twentieth-century fortifications. A trilingual handbook of Atlantic Wall installations is not an update of Virilio's meditation on total war but a guide for ramblers.[33] The inventories of bunker designs, grid references, photographic documentation and logistical and administrative background collected in these volumes provides a staggering level of detail, placing twentieth-century military fortifications on a footing with steam railways and classic cars, with their own esoteric terminology – Lincolnshire three-bay, Dover Quad, Pickett-Hamilton Fort, Essex Lozenge – and rarity value.

The military bunker has become an established component of the 'enrichment', 'dark' or war tourist's itinerary, with conventional tourist expectations such as beautiful surroundings also catered for since many military installations were deliberately built in remote or secluded areas. The Hack Green Secret Nuclear Bunker in Nantwich, for example, promises views of 'the picturesque farmland and rolling Cheshire countryside', but reminds visitors that 'it was not always like this!' The incongruity of exposed 'secret' military installations is patently a large part of their attraction, and the jarring collision of rolling countryside and high-tech bunkers produces an uncanny effect of

LANDSCAPE AS WEAPON

insecure security, a suspension of everyday domestic life that at the same time attempts to domesticate that which threatens it. It is this irreducible awkwardness of military remains that is captured by the English Heritage website's description of the York Cold War Bunker as the organization's 'most modern and spine-chilling' property. Visitors are advised not to miss the decontamination room.

The preservation and education agendas are, unsurprisingly, heavily foregrounded in the promotional materials of sites funded with government money. While this is clearly intended to neutralize the more troubling aspects of the existence of the sites and their intended functions, the 'spine-chilling' dimension is inevitably also part of the equation, and an attraction that eviscerates completely the claustrophobic and frightening attributes of a military site is unlikely to succeed in its educational or recreational mission. Part of the mechanism of reassurance provided for the visitor, as well as the contextual gesture towards familiar and relaxing landscape and the reminders of how things are no longer dangerous, is the self-reflexive strategy of narrating the process through which the site has been rescued from abandonment. This not only serves to show how money has been spent but recuperates the site as part of the ongoing process of making secure previously amorphous threats. The Liverpool War Museum website, for example, includes photographs of the Western Approaches bunker in its 'derelict state' and in its current, reconstructed condition. An integral part of the narrative of the site's history, then, is redemptive: the disturbingly invisible has been made safe for view.

The problem with this process of retrieval is that it serves to gut the site of the awful connotations that make it historically relevant in the first place. The irony is not lost even on the archaeologist John Schofield, whose job it is to identify military sites for English Heritage preservation and who has published widely on the practical and theoretical aspects of defence heritage. Schofield concedes that it is 'the places without funding or conservation [that] are often also the most evocative'.[34] While Schofield is understandably invested in presenting the case for saving bunkers and other sites, and draws on a range of strategies, including the relevance of artistic interventions, to demonstrate how such places are culturally important, the implicit violence at the heart of any military installation, however smartly it is renovated, remains unresolved. It is violence that is evoked at the non-conserved sites in all its complex and affective forms; it may also be violence that is evoked at retrofitted tourist bunkers, but now it is violence mediated by the apparatus of recreation and heritage. As Don DeLillo writes in his epic exploration of the Cold War's legacy, *Underworld* (1997), tourists 'travel somewhere not for museums and sunsets but for ruins, bombed-out terrain, for the moss-grown memory of torture and war'.[35] In other words, the modern tourist wants an aestheticized violence generated by the awkward combination of the authentic and the picturesque.

It is worth remembering that the National Trust decided not to demolish the pagodas at Orford Ness in the early 1990s; this awareness of what one of the British defence preservation studies calls the 'fearsome heritage' of conflict gives many otherwise unremarkable sites powerful ambient clout. Increasingly, artists and other cultural workers are less likely to deal with military buildings as found material and will more probably be funded for residencies and installations by the owner or custodian of a decommissioned site.[36] In this way, while serious and powerful work may still result, as in Louise K. Wilson's projects at Orford Ness and Spadeadam, the extent to which this kind of institutionalized 'intervention' into militarized space normalizes the bunker-as-artwork is not unproblematic.[37]

The retrofitting of Second World War bunkers and the unveiling of Cold War installations demonstrates the success of the military in being able to conceal itself from public view. The authority of the new tourist site lies in its capacity to demonstrate the way in which military secrets can be withdrawn and revealed at will. The tourist bunker is a spectacle of covert operations; showing the facility exposes our previous ignorance of its existence, and the belated invitation to view is predicated on its current uselessness. One of the implications here is that it is only safe for the public to know about things that are effectively redundant. The liberty to restore a bunker as a museum or gallery and the ingenuity with which concealed or feared sites of terror have been recuperated as spaces of cultural speculation is a freedom to enter and look upon what is constructed as a lost world. In some ways, to paraphrase Caruth, the preservation of the bunker has made all too bearable the nature of its survival.

On the other hand, just as Virilio's Atlantic Wall project provides a way of looking askance at Cold War secrecy and war memorials appropriate the architecture of aggression as a modality of mourning, it may be that even in its commodified forms the bunker retains its power to speak, with all its dumb force, of an undiminished oscillation between the crisis of life and the crisis of death. As the relics of twentieth-century conflict are preserved, memorialized and retooled, Virilio's point that 'the new fortress' is underfoot and invisible is confirmed in the deployment of sewers, tunnels and other subterranean bunkered spaces of what Simon Guy calls the 'shadow architecture' of twenty-first-century conflict.[38] Security anxieties about the prevalence of concealed underground weapons facilities replay the fears of the Cold War while the utilization of caves and complex tunnel systems by terrorists and border-crossing migrants also continues to defy high-tech surveillance systems. The failure to extract Osama bin Laden from the cave complex he was believed to have constructed at Tora Bora, despite the use of the optimistically named 'bunker-buster' bombs, suggests the continuing capacity of the bunker to frustrate assault and its persistence as an ambivalent site of cultural and military anxiety.[39] In the case of Bin Laden, the bunker complex was no more than a conjuration of the u.s. military, indicative of a mindset struggling to conceive of an enemy not locatable in a fortified den.

Defunct bunkers, however imbricated in economic and cultural systems of affirmation, still work as surrogates for the real but unknowable systems of security and governance that continue to shape the limits of what can be exposed and documented. As restrictions on photography become more widespread and public space becomes increasingly monitored and managed by private interests deploying a discourse of security to discipline and regulate populations, the attention paid to the bunkers of previous conflicts begins to emerge as a mode of oblique critical interrogation and an expression of persistent and deep ambivalence. That which can be seen, occupied and modified stands as a necessary substitute for that which remains aloof, spectral and threatening. While it could be argued that this substitution is precisely what is achieved by the renovation of sites of aggression by the heritage business, the stubborn fact of the bunker as, to recall Sebald, a 'monolithic, monstrous incarnation of ugliness and blind violence' refuses, in the end, to yield to the seductions of the military–industrial–leisure complex. It is this very blankness, its double valence as refuge and tomb, that has made the bunker an embodiment of so many of the twentieth century's horrors. The disturbing and

LANDSCAPE AS WEAPON

relentless oscillation between life and death, ruin and rubble, nature and culture, exposure and concealment, image and object, art and atrocity that vibrates deep in the rebars of the bunker's reinforced concrete is the tremor of modernity's ambivalence no amount of cultural recuperation can, or should, contain.

Nevertheless, as part of the infrastructure of the leisure industry, the kind of shock often registered by writers and artists when apprehending bunkers has, to a considerable extent, been absorbed by the pacifying narratives that support their preservation. The respect which Second World War and Cold War sites now enjoy as places of archaeological, historical and memorial interest has no doubt been hard won, but the problem with legitimacy is that it can close down antagonistic interpretations that make such places relevant. Much like other modern ruins that have become the material for ruin porn, thinking about military installations must now also involve a critical interrogation of their overdetermined status in the culture.[40] Without a reflexive awareness of the bunker's relevance to contemporary discourses of secrecy and security, the danger is that the restored or protected remains of military sites will function merely to distance and cordon off the frightening implications of their existence as past times. What Virilio and others identified in the bunker is its capacity to generate what Foucault calls a history of the present and to gesture towards invisible continuations of its legacy. Part of that legacy, it now seems, is the spectacle of power the bunker performs in its afterlife as icon of, and venue for, displaced fantasies of military aggression. Heritage itself – as an idea and an industry – has become not only a primary mediator of the bunker's historical significance, but an intrinsic part of the bunker's intolerable history. As such, the management of military sites as heritage oscillates dangerously between offering a critical interrogation of those sites and reiterating military power's capacity for display as a mode of concealment. It is now, perhaps, not only the unbearable story of the event that requires attention, but what is most pressing is a radical rethinking of the unbearable story of its survival.

Too Bright for Unshielded Eyes

The bunker has become an overground attraction in post-Cold War Europe and elsewhere, allowing for a partial performative revelation of what was once hidden. While part of the fascination with once-active military installations is no doubt related to the dubious affective significance attributed to spaces of awesome violence, such sites do provide an opportunity, as I think Virilio senses, by means of indirection, to rehearse an encounter with the apparatus of an otherwise concealed power. It is part of the peculiarity of the bunker's cultural position that it is its lumpen, immovable redundancy that speaks of another, hidden and unknowable power that cannot be seen or touched. The bunker that can now be seen suggests to us other bunkers as yet unknown.

This quality of misdirection, intrinsic to the visual economy of modern warfare and security, does mean that there is little prospect of addressing or representing power directly. For this reason, the most successful attempts to grasp the extent to which the landscape has been captured by military power tend to be those that are able to see beyond the relics of the military–industrial past. Indeed, to fully recognize the militarization of contemporary life it might be necessary to, in a sense, look the other way.

This is precisely what is achieved, I think, in a curious book published in 1984 by the celebrated American non-fiction writer John McPhee, *La Place de la Concorde Suisse*. So well camouflaged by its title is the subject of this book that the British publisher,

Faber, decided to rename it *The Swiss Army*, presumably in the hope that the work might gain readers by rendering visible its contents. Yet the opacity of the title is entirely to the point, since McPhee's book, as the opening line makes clear, is about radical indirection: 'The Swiss have not fought a war for nearly five hundred years, and are determined to know how so as not to.'[41] *La Place de la Concorde Suisse* is McPhee's account of time spent with the Section de Renseignements, the information patrol in a unit of the Tenth Mountain Division of the Swiss Army. Famously neutral, Switzerland nonetheless maintains robust and battle-ready armed forces, drawing the majority of its military personnel through compulsory service. It was the Swiss concept of a fighting nation – what McPhee cites at one point as the Swiss self-description as a country with 'an aptitude for war'[42] – that provided the model for the Israeli Defense Forces.[43]

The Swiss Army, as McPhee observes, is a 'civilian army', and most of the time its soldiers are to be found 'walking around in street clothes or in blue from the collar down'.[44] Writing for a U.S. audience – and more specifically, for readers of the *New Yorker*, where McPhee's book began as a series of articles published in 1983 – the author explains that Switzerland is twice the size of New Jersey and much less densely populated than that state. In order to underscore precisely what this might mean socially, McPhee adds: 'If you understand the New York Yacht Club, the Cosmos Club, the Metropolitan Club, the Century Club, the Piedmont Driving Club, you would understand the Swiss Army.'[45] In other words, the Swiss Army is a private social club where all eligible men under fifty are members.

The point of McPhee's comparison between elite American social networks and the Swiss Army is not just to provide a condescending sense of scale in order to be able to position the

Swiss as globally anachronistic in military terms, but to signal the thoroughgoing integration of business and military affairs in Switzerland. More broadly, and in the context of the first term of Ronald Reagan's presidency (1981–4), during which time McPhee researched and published his book, *La Place de la Concorde Suisse* serves as an oblique commentary on the military definition of reality as it was being shaped by Reagan's massive increase in military spending and revived Cold War rhetoric. McPhee does not once mention American domestic or foreign policy because he does not have to; his account of a nation that has seamlessly knitted together financial and military power – the fortress-like security of Swiss banks, McPhee notes, 'is emphasized by the Swiss Army'[46] – to the point where it shapes the entire fabric of society is at once peculiarly foreign and disquietingly familiar. 'The army,' observes McPhee of the Swiss example, 'in addition to all its other functions, has long been considered a first-rate school of business management . . . The special training required for a position on the general staff is looked upon as the equivalent of two years at the Harvard Business School.'[47] Swiss banks, he concludes with one last nod to his American readers, are the closest counterpart the country has to West Point.[48] The business of war and war as business in Switzerland cannot fail, here, to resonate with contemporary u.s. affairs.

The name 'La Place de la Concorde Suisse' does not refer to a grand public square but to what McPhee calls a 'frozen intersection' of glacier streams – 'a world too bright for unshielded eyes' – beneath a range of towering mountain peaks 'where all horizons are violent'.[49] In 1857 the British Alpine mountaineer Rev. J. F. Hardy called this spot 'the Place de la Concorde of Nature; wherever you look there is a grand road and a lofty dome'.[50] For McPhee, it is here that the 'place that will never

LANDSCAPE AS WEAPON

need defending represents what the Swiss defend'.[51] McPhee's title, then, designates a fusion of the natural and cultural, a site of geomorphological splendour that borrows its name from opulent Parisian urban design. It is a crossroads and a paradox, folding, as does its French namesake, intimations of terror and conciliation (built for a king in 1755, what was originally called Place Louis XV later served as the site for public executions during the Revolution before being renamed Place de la Concorde in 1795). Hardy was no doubt looking for a human analogue for divine creation when he saw Paris in the Alps; what McPhee sees (or is dazzled by) is a collaboration of nature and nation that converges along the violent horizon of peaceful (non)aggression.

At 60 per cent alpine, Switzerland is indeed a natural fortress, though it is a nature thoroughly managed over centuries in order to appear untouched; the Swiss, writes McPhee, 'have not embarrassed their terrain'.[52] Instead, they have mastered the art of camouflage. The Rhône valley, for example, he explains, has airstrips but no airport, no 'evident' hangars or planes, but 'If one just happens to be looking . . . one might see a mountain open – might see something like an enormous mousehole appear chimerically at the base of an alp. Out of the mountain comes a supersonic aircraft.'[53] Offering some of the most picturesque and most heavily photographed landscapes in the world, Switzerland, for McPhee, is nature ironized. There is 'scarcely a scene' in the country, he writes, 'that would not sell a calendar [and] there is scarcely a scene that is not ready to erupt in fire to repel an invasive war'. Pilots sit inside mountains waiting to scramble; the airstrips do not appear on maps though they are plain to see, 'like Band-Aids all over the Alps'; there are forest clearings that 'make no sense'.[54] The military presence is curiously obvious and denied, enigmatic, chimerical, yet at the same time banal and beyond remark. Townspeople go about their business while soldiers conduct war games in their midst. 'As any tourist can testify,' notes McPhee, 'the Swiss Army is probably the most visible army in the world.'[55] The military is so visible that it disappears.

For McPhee, Switzerland is a hollowed-out country, rustic scenery theatrically concealing networks of tunnels, weapons caches, hospitals, a year's worth of fuel for the army and regularly replenished food supplies; some sites are secret even within the army.[56] It is a nation of locked doors and dead ends, of 'weapons and soldiers under barns', 'cannons under pretty houses'.[57] There are firing ranges everywhere – 'Shooting rifles is a national sport. It is also compulsory'[58] – and military equipment, including guns, are kept at home, ready to use at short notice. In addition to large public bomb shelters, all new houses are required to include a fallout shelter. Not only is Switzerland calmly duplicitous, it is also ready to blow: 'every railroad and highway tunnel has been prepared to pinch shut explosively' and often, 'the civilian engineer who created the bridge will, in his capacity as a military officer, be given the task of planning its destruction.'[59] Here, as everywhere in McPhee's Switzerland, creation and destruction reside together.

This is, of course, the world the Cold War made, and the inseparability of civilian and military life, while certainly exaggerated in the case of Switzerland, was not exclusive to it. The strategy of indirection McPhee uses to show this militarized concealment replicates the duplicity of the Swiss landscape and the paradox upon which his book turns, that the place that never fights is the most heavily militarized, captures something of what, in retrospect, seems like the profound oddness of the Cold War mentality. It may be that the recent fascination with redundant military installations is partly about working through the ramifications of that oddness, the strangeness of an aftermath for which there was no (obvious) battle. The real lesson of the Cold War, though, is that there is nothing that is not part of the conflict and that nothing is necessarily what it seems to be. The military installations of the Cold War, in their implacable blankness, stand as reminders of the ways in which that conflict, perhaps more than any other, achieved the naturalization of dishonesty and dissimulation.

5

The General Was Rubbish in the End

On the evening of Monday 21 August 2018, 250 people gathered in McCorkle Place on the campus of the University of North Carolina at Chapel Hill. Behind a makeshift screen made out of a series of tall banners, protestors attached ropes and pulled to the ground the statue of a Confederate soldier that had stood there since 1913. The statue, known as Silent Sam, was among many memorials to the Confederate dead and the Confederate cause that have, in recent years, and especially since the murder by a white suprem-acist of nine black churchgoers in Charleston, South Carolina, in June 2015, become the focus of protest against the persistence of racism in the United States. On 12 August 2017, during a far-right protest against the proposed removal of a statue of Confederate General Robert E. Lee from a park in Charlottesville, Virginia, a Nazi sympathizer drove his car into a crowd of counter-protestors, killing one person and injuring a number of others. Two days after the violence in Charlottesville, a monument to Confederate soldiers known as 'Old Joe' was removed from downtown Gainesville, Florida, and in Durham, North Carolina, protestors toppled a statue of a Confederate soldier in front of the Durham county courthouse. On 19 August Duke University removed a Robert E. Lee statue from Duke Chapel. Similar removals took place during August 2017 in the cities of Baltimore and Annapolis in Maryland and in Austin, Texas.

There was nothing remarkable about Silent Sam, and it was the very ordinariness of the statue that made it, and the hundreds of other monuments to the Confederacy that remain in towns and cities across much of the United States, so offensive. It is a measure of the frustration felt at the unwillingness of officials to address local laws and regulations preventing the simple removal of statues in many places that causes crowds to gather to do the job themselves. Though official removal of statues is rarely uncontentious – the workers charged with removing four monuments in New Orleans in April 2015 wore flak jackets and were guarded by police – the violent taking down of statues is often the exasperated response to years of official inertia.

The temporality of public monuments is contradictory. On one hand, the motivation for the erection of a public monument is shaped by a desire to extend across time the virtue perceived to be enshrined and commemorated in the monument. Furthermore, the public nature of the monument assumes, and sometimes even demands, that the values embodied in the monument should be shared. As such, the erection of a monument is a commitment to continuity, not only across time and into the future, but across and through the community. The installation of a material marker means to hold the line and speak to all comers. On the other hand, this claim upon the future and upon the community almost instantaneously becomes anachronistic, since the frozen moment held in place by the stone, marble or bronze is always backward-looking and, as time passes, incrementally out of step with the world around it. The claim to permanence is rarely respected for long. The permanence, Andreas Huyssen writes, 'promised by a monument in stone is always built on quicksand'.[1] Statues are easily toppled; more frequently, they are simply ignored.

Herein lies another paradoxical aspect of the public monument: something intended to announce itself and what it stands for very quickly becomes functionally invisible due precisely to its immovability. Robert Musil, writing in Vienna in 1927, reflected that, despite being 'erected to be seen', monuments are 'impregnated with something that repels attention, causing the glance to roll right off'. Monuments, he concludes, are 'conspicuously inconspicuous', the most invisible thing in the world.[2] The same is true, for Musil, of the memorial function of the monument, which rarely makes itself known. Intended to grab the attention, instead monuments 'repel the very thing that they are supposed to attract'.[3]

The general ineffectiveness of the public monument, for Musil, renders them little more than grotesque relics that, if noticed at all, are likely to be greeted with a shudder, 'as you do beside the walls of a madhouse'.[4] This is especially true, he claims, if the sculpture is of a general or prince, frozen in an absurd pose, ready for action but never following through.

> His flag is waving in his hand, and there's no wind. His sword is drawn and no one draws back in fear. . . . By God, the figures in monuments never make a move and yet remain forever frozen in a faux pas. It is a desperate situation.[5]

The triumph of statuary is, for Musil, entirely negative, since the irrelevance of the monument is such that as soon as someone is thus memorialized, they are safely cast 'into the sea of oblivion'.[6]

Musil is half right. The ineffectiveness of the public monument as a statement of permanent relevance is clear and the folly of such gestures only rightly dismissed. This is, for Musil, a relief, since the aggressive demands made by the monument, the way it takes command and defines its surroundings, would otherwise be a genuine threat. If a monument is to achieve the kind of permanence its sponsors presumably desire, it must be achieved at the cost of its relevance. A monument to someone or some cause no one remembers or cares about will last for ever; it will exist like a tree, bench or lamp post or, if it is big enough, serve as a landmark or a roundabout. It will survive but it will cease to matter.

There is, however, more to the monument than its built-in obsolescence, as the case of Silent Sam and other contested sites suggest. The shrinking of relevance into invisibility might explain why objectionable statues survive as long as they do, but an upsurge in iconoclasm gives the lie to the notion of invisibility, or at least indicates that what might have dissolved into street furniture for some has remained a material signifier of oppression for others. It is here that the permanence of the monument must be recognized as not merely a function of the narcissism or misplaced universalism of its sponsors, but as a bid to command not just the physical site upon which the statue stands, but the future into which it steadfastly advances.

For film-maker Mark Lewis, commenting on Soviet monuments, public works of art invariably serve as a means of 'marking out and policing the public sphere'.[7] He thinks Musil underestimates 'the continued efficacy of the monument in its ability to be always more and less than the figure which it ostensibly represents'. This capacity to be more and less than it appears means that the monument's 'invisibility is a sign of a silent interpellation', a subtle but pervasive control of space and meaning.[8] What Musil sees as the monument's ineffective silence and invisibility, Lewis reads as intrinsic to their space-defining power. For this reason, Lewis insists that the monument remains a marker of domination precisely because of its purported invisibility. During periods of social crisis, uprisings, rebellions and revolutions, public monuments become targets for symbolic violence, removal or destruction not because they have been ignored, but because they cannot be ignored.

Here, the movement between the invisible and the visible, the permanent and transitory – the unstable qualities that sceptics of public monuments claim are the reasons why the erection of such monuments is pointless – becomes vital as the pointlessly immobile statue is animated by forces in the present motivated to challenge, through an assault on the object itself, the values invested in it in the past. As Lewis writes, 'we need to acknowledge that the *visibility* which inaugurates such an attack [on the monument] is a pre-requisite for any attempt to re-interpret and intervene within this area of the symbolic realm.'[9] In other words, not only does iconoclasm make visible the monument as a site of power, but the monument must already be rendered visible in order that the assault can proceed. The invisibility of the monument that Musil mistakes for its irrelevance is therefore seen, here, as a mode of concealment that must be overturned. Seeing the monument for what it is can then lead to a direct challenge to the symbolic power it represents. This act of critical unveiling gives the lie to the notion of the harmless monument that is merely a relic from a past no longer remembered.

Show Me the Man You Honour

It is easier to find examples of how much statues are hated than accounts of their splendour. This is undoubtedly due to the frequently unwelcome display of power shown by those who like to erect statues, not to mention the claims that may be enshrined in the statue itself. 'Show me the man you honour,' wrote Thomas Carlyle in 1850: 'I know by that symptom, better than by any other, what kind of man you yourself are.'[10] Over a century later, John Berger echoed this sentiment when he wrote that 'A state can be judged by the future its sculpture sets out to promise it.'[11] Public sculpture does not merely serve a memorial function here but pushes out into and seeks to define the world to come. This sense of an inextricable relationship between art and state is there at the beginning of the discipline of art history, in Johann Winckelmann's 1764 *History of Ancient Art*, which systemically analysed Greek, Greco-Roman and Roman art as the articulation of a civilization's rise and decline. For Winckelmann, the artistic achievements of the classical world are inseparable from its political institutions and its geography; in other words, it is through its context, its associations, that sculpture gains what value it might have: great sculpture is produced by great civilizations. It is due to Winckelmann, as Michael North argues, 'that so many cultural histories rely on sculpture as a major category of evidence, using it as a social diagnostic, an unfailing key to the health of the society that produced it'. As such, monuments become 'microcosmic summations of entire cultures'.[12]

Winckelmann's influence in the late eighteenth century shaped the Neoclassical commitment to the perfection of the Greek system of government – a system where respect for art is the cornerstone of the state. This is nowhere more evident than in the public monuments built by the emerging democracies of the late eighteenth and early nineteenth centuries, not least in Washington, DC. A good example is Horatio Greenough's 30-ton figure of 'Enthroned Washington' (1832), commissioned by Congress to sit in the rotunda of the Capitol building and modelled on one of the Seven Wonders of the Ancient World, the great statue of Zeus at Olympia. The grand aspiration, however, was misplaced, and Greenough's Washington, when it arrived in DC in 1841, generated enough controversy and criticism that the half-naked statue was relocated to the east lawn of the Capitol in 1843. This was still not far enough out of the way, so in 1908 the statue was transferred to the Smithsonian Castle, where it stayed until 1964, when it was moved to the second floor of what is now the National Museum of American History. People clearly found it impossible to fold real American democrats into the history of ideal forms, though Washington, DC, is full of attempts to do just that.

The problem with 'Enthroned Washington' may have focused on the embarrassing vision of the president in classical costume, but there is also a deeper discomfort registered here about the very legitimacy of monuments in a democracy. John Quincy Adams famously wrote that democracy has no monuments, strikes no medals and bears no head of a man on its coins. The thing about statues, as we have seen, is that they fix the object they represent and as such appear to make permanent and freeze the concepts and values they enshrine. In so doing, statues preserve but at the same time make inaccessible those concepts and values, locking down into marble or bronze what might otherwise be living ideas and actions open to change and transformation. Public monuments, as Kirk Savage writes, 'are an inherently conservative art form' that 'obey the logic of the last word, the logic of closure'.[13] Any monument to democracy, then, threatens to ossify the living form it represents.

Thinking about statues, as well as providing models for ideal orders, also invites consideration of the way the statue provides what Kenneth Gross calls 'an image of the fate of living concepts,

Horatio Greenough, *Enthroned Washington*, 1840, marble.

ideas, and fantasies, an image of their being calcified, codified, hollowed out, or made stupid'.[14] The statue, Gross continues, 'provides an image of ideas made into exclusive laws or habits, transformed into agents of compulsion or forms of blank mystery. The statue represents an idea that has been silenced, restricted, or censored, even by virtue of its formal eloquence.'[15] For Gross, the statue directs us to three 'images of fate': the fate of authority, of 'living and acting persons' and of bodies. In each case, while the statue supposedly secures that fate in substantive form, it acts as a kind of threat, reminding us that the very attempt at preservation is likely to fail. The statue refuses decay and death but in doing so functions as a double for the cadavers we non-statues will inevitably become. In short, then, statues call attention to issues of power, history and death, but rarely with the assurance that their bold presence is supposed to ensure.

While the classical model of statuary appears to promise nobility and transcendence, the reality is more complex and difficult. But though the statue may not provide an incarnation of an ideal order and unity between art and state, what it does do, *contra* Musil, is draw attention towards itself; the statue is, as Gross explains, 'the definer of axes of view, centers of attention, and fixities of memory, the anchor of what is volatile, the guardian of what is ready to flee'.[16] The puzzle, then, is that the statue is both invisible and glaringly visible, a naturalized presence and therefore unnoticed, yet also aggressively in place. It is precisely this ambiguity that makes public sculpture a complex form, seemingly able to satisfy contradictory requirements: to be there and not there at the same time, to threaten and to mourn, to elevate and bring to earth, to remind and to be forgotten.

This ambiguity Henry James took to be duplicity. In *The American Scene* (1903), James reflects on the notional authority of Augustus Saint-Gaudens's gaudy equestrian statue of General Sherman in Central Park, New York City. The image presented of Sherman the 'Destroyer', for James, is hopelessly compromised by the contradictory political work it is being asked to do. On one side, he writes, the image of 'an overwhelming military advance', all heroic strain and billowing drapery, is 'splendidly rendered'. At the same time, though, the idea is presented that 'the Destroyer is a messenger of peace, with the olive branch too waved in the blast and with the embodied grace, in the form of a beautiful American girl, attending his business.' The unsatisfactory result, for James, is to 'confound destroyers with benefactors'. The dishonesty of the Sherman statue is that it refuses to have what James thinks monuments ought to have: 'a clean, clear meaning'. James wants Sherman depicted as 'deadly and terrible', 'crested not with peace, but with snakes'. He should not radiate benevolence but, 'by every ingenious device, the misery, the ruin and the vengeance of his track'. Although James admits it is not his affair to teach the artist 'how such horrors may be monumentally signified', it is enough, he insists, 'that their having been perpetrated is the very ground of the monument'.[17]

Current campaigns to remove statues celebrating racists and imperialists, in the U.S. and beyond, would no doubt agree with James that it is a flagrant misrepresentation of history to present killers as saviours. James wants a destroyer to look like one, though his stark conclusion suggests that the presence of any statue at all signifies the horrors the monument dishonestly refuses to admit.

The Gipper

While Greenough's Washington did not manage to stay in the Capitol building for long, there is no shortage of statues there.

The National Statuary Hall, built to resemble an ancient amphi-theatre and for fifty years the meeting place of the House of Representatives, is devoted to sculptures of prominent Americans. The first statue was placed there in 1870 and by 1971 all fifty states had contributed at least one; by 1990 all but five states had con-tributed two. In addition to the great Americans, the Hall also permanently houses Enrico Causici's Neoclassical plaster *Liberty and the Eagle* (1817–19) and the *Car of History* (1819) by Carlo Franzoni, depicting Clio, Muse of History, riding in the chariot of Time (the wheel of which, in a display of unashamed Neoclassical kitsch, is a clock face). While all the state statues were originally in the hall, since the collection has grown new additions have had to oust sitting tenants for space. In 2009 Ronald Reagan entered Statuary Hall at the expense of Civil War-era Californian minister and politician Thomas Starr King. At the dedication, former White House chief of staff James Baker said that the Reagan statue 'will stand forever as a silent sentry in these hallowed halls, to teach our children and our grandchildren about that which once was and to inspire them with visions of that which can be again – today, tomorrow and unto the generations'.[18] Or at least until Reagan is replaced by someone else.

Reagan's entry into the Capitol's pantheon of heroes anticipated a rash of Reagan effigies and other monuments that were unveiled in and outside the U.S. during 2011, the centenary of Reagan's birth. Among the commemorations, a memorial mass was held in Krakow, a street was renamed after Reagan in Prague and his name was also given to a roundabout in Lublin, eastern Poland. On 29 June, a 2.1 m (7 ft) bronze statue of Reagan was unveiled in Budapest, and a few days later, on 4 July, London followed with a 3 m (10 ft) statue outside the American Embassy in Grosvenor Square. These memorials join the statue already erected in

2007 in Warsaw and other international dedications, including a Grenadian commemorative stamp collection and the Ronald Reagan Ballistic Missile Defense Test Site in the Marshall Islands. In the U.S. itself there are more than one hundred dedications to Reagan, from preserved Cold War installations like the Ronald Reagan Minuteman Missile Site in Cooperstown, North Dakota, to educational institutions such as the Ronald Reagan Fundamental School in Yuma, Arizona, post offices, roads, bridges, airports and fields (there is a Ronald Reagan Spirit of America Field in Decatur, Alabama). The Ronald Reagan Legacy Project, an organization that aims to have one substantial thing named after Reagan in each state and in each county in the U.S., has been instrumental in promoting many of these dedications and seeking to encourage states to recognize Reagan's birthday, 6 February, as Reagan Day.

The centenary statues of Reagan, the president most adept at mobilizing nostalgia for a simpler time, are not only themselves susceptible to a certain longing for the heroics of the 1980s, but, formally, return the memorial to the figurative conventions of statuary that have, since the 1980s, been in decline. The attributes of the Reagan statues insist upon, as convention dictates, the phallic verticality of the individual depicted; an attention to capturing the likeness of the subject; the plinth as elevator of the singular individual as noble and triumphant, worthy of memorialization; and a de facto absence of context – the figure stands alone, without clues as to why he is there. The white male body, bronzed and permanent, is enough. The Reagan statues are not about history but about myth. As Garry Wills writes regarding the Reagan world view: 'The stories about our past were always better than any evidence about it'; for Reagan, America was 'suspended between two glowing myths: the religious past and the technological future'.[19] Reagan presented himself to the nation as the kind of American that many thought had been swept away by the 1960s; he was patriarchal, authoritative, protective, patriotic, unpretentious, uncultured and more comfortable on the sports field or on a horse than in an office. From a critical point of view, Reagan was a cliché of post-war masculinity just like the characters he had once played in Hollywood films. Yet not only was this the Reagan many voted for, it was the Reagan subsequently enshrined as the president who 'won' the Cold War. To a significant extent, history has accepted the version of Reagan he himself had always performed. Furthermore, in retrospect and in comparison to the privileged ineptitude of George W. Bush and the grotesque parody of patriotism presented by Donald Trump, Reagan has been treated kindly by recent history, regardless of the part he himself played in making the Bush and Trump years possible.

Ronald Reagan statues are not exclusively to be found outside the United States, but while the overseas Reagan is largely depicted in the business suit of the international leader, at home, he is just as likely to be represented as the cowboy president. The Ronald Reagan Memorial Library in California and the National Cowboy and Western Heritage Museum in Oklahoma City hold identical bronzes of Reagan in cowboy gear, and in Rapid City, South Dakota (known as the city of the presidents), where there is a statue of every president dotted around the streets, the Reagan statue is again a cowboy. This is not the Neoclassicism of Greenough's Washington, but the cowboy clothes might be seen as an updated version, with the mythic West substituting for the ideals of antiquity. The union of the aesthetic and the political is still at work here, the cowboy president signifying the values of American democracy. Is this nobility in the sense that it might have been conceived in classical statuary, or merely a debased form of hero worship?

In his polemic 'Hudson's Statue' (1850), Carlyle uses the proposed raising of a statue in honour of George Hudson, the so-called railway king, to bemoan a collective imagination unable to distinguish heroes from hucksters and willing to throw up memorials in honour of all manner of adventurers and opportunists. This is the danger of letting people decide things for themselves. Carlyle's disturbing hostility towards democracy is plain, though his impatience with a historical sense so impoverished that it embraces every aggressive entrepreneur or politician as a candidate for the bronze memorial treatment remains pertinent. The problem with democracy, for Carlyle, is that its concerns are so prosaic. Where is the shared purpose and collective sense of identity that might generate a monument that speaks to the nobility of the democratic project? Maybe the problem with the Reagan cowboy statues is that he is not on a horse.

The Noble Rider

There are two Reagan statues in his boyhood home of Dixon, Illinois, one outside the house where he once lived, erected in 1988 and representing the adult Reagan admiring corn kernels in his hand. A second, more recent statue of a mounted Reagan was dedicated in Dixon in 2009. It is called *Begins the Trail*, based on a photo of youthful 1950s Reagan wearing a T-shirt. Since Plato's *Phaedrus*, if not before, the image of a man riding a horse has been part of a powerful cultural myth of human elevation, mastery and nobility. This mythical image involves a human harnessing a natural energy with all its intelligence, violence and beauty. The equestrian statue is about holding steady but also about mobile power. The horse is also another pedestal, the rider in a sense raised twice in the statue even as the horse and rider are made one in the unity of the bronze or marble. The purpose of an equestrian statue is invariably to remind us of the nobility of the rider and of statues themselves.

In his Princeton address of 1942, published as 'The Noble Rider and the Sound of Words', poet Wallace Stevens begins by quoting Plato's description of the soul as a charioteer drawn by winged horses. For Plato, the Charioteer represents intellect or reason, guiding the chariot towards truth. One horse is of noble breed, representing the positive part of passionate nature, and the other is wilder, representing irrational passions and appetites. We soar with such images, says Stevens, but then 'droop in our flight' because we remember that chariots and charioteers no longer exist. 'We are not free to yield ourselves' to the nobility of the poetry and the 'imagination loses vitality as it ceases to adhere to what is real'.[20] While we might understand Plato's figure, Stevens goes on, we do not 'participate in it' because it is unreal to us; imagination 'has the strength of reality or none at all'.[21] In order to pursue the possibility of nobility in the present and find the contemporary equivalent of Plato's charioteer, Stevens moves from Don Quixote through Renaissance statuary to the equestrian statue of President Andrew Jackson in Lafayette Square in Washington, DC. He is not, however, impressed. 'This is a work of fancy,' Stevens flatly concludes, reminding the reader of Coleridge's distinction between imagination and fancy. Imagination is vital, creative and transformative, while fancy is mechanical and accepts things much as they are. The Jackson statue, for Stevens, in its ordinariness and conventionality, is evidence of how 'easily satisfied' the American will has turned out to be 'in its efforts to realize itself in knowing itself'.[22]

For Stevens, statues represent a static, solid and fixed mode of representation and are therefore antithetical to the kind of

Donald L. Reed's bronze statue *Begins the Trail*, unveiled in Dixon, Illinois, in 2009.

Bronze version from 1926 of James Earle Fraser's *The End of the Trail* in Shaler Park in Waupun, Wisconsin.

fluid and mobile energy he believed should characterize the contemporary moment. The fixed form of the statue, especially in its official, monumental mode, represents the state as domineering and inflexible, indifferent and unconnected to the life going on around it. The statue of Jackson, for Stevens, fails to produce the sense of nobility it strives for and, as such, the journey from Plato to Jackson is a movement of loss. The statue in DC has nothing to say that is not already known, as far as Stevens is concerned; its main function is to reveal the national character to itself, and that character is one bereft of curiosity or insight. Here, Stevens seems to echo Alexis de Tocqueville, who saw the American desire for monumentality as compensation for the poverty of character in a democracy: 'Nowhere else do the citizens seem smaller than in a democratic nation, and nowhere else does the nation itself seem greater, so that it is easily conceived as a vast picture.'[23]

In *Begins the Trail* the youthful Reagan is offered as the soul of the nation: the cowboy as noble rider. But the title of the Dixon statue must remind us of another, more famous equestrian statue, which the Reagan statue responds to but also seems to attempt to refigure. This is *The End of the Trail* by James Earle Fraser, a 7.6 m (25 ft) plaster statue of a defeated Native American that won the prestigious Panama-Pacific International Exposition in San Francisco in 1915. Due to the scarcity of bronze during wartime, the sculpture was not recast but abandoned in a mud pit until it was retrieved in 1919 and relocated to Mooney Grove Park, in Visalia, California. There it stood for fifty years and was later cast in bronze for the Cowboy Hall of Fame in 1969. *The End of the Trail* has become an iconic image, reproduced in thousands of photographs and adorning everything from calendars to postcards and ashtrays. It became synonymous with

Vietnam-era melancholy and a hippy icon, famously used by The Beach Boys on the cover of *Surf's Up*, the 1971 album that saw the band looking to reimagine their conventionally optimistic image for more dour times.

The End of the Trail, as if in critical response to the Lafayette Square Jackson, the slave owner and ethnic cleanser, memorializes the destruction of Native Americans, the close of the frontier and the end of an era of American history already heavily larded with myth. *Begins the Trail* is resolutely a work of optimism that both rewinds the clock to present Reagan as the youth who will become president and replaces Fraser's worn-out and bedraggled Native American with a robust clean-cut WASP. *Begins the Trail* achieves in statuary what Reagan sought to achieve in national politics: an erasure of the negativity of the 1960s and a return to frontier simplicity and patriarchal values. *The End of the Trail* became kitsch; *Begins the Trail* starts as kitsch. If Stevens is right, the presiding function of the statue is to stand for the failure of imagination. The statue is always, for Stevens, about death.

In 'An Ordinary Evening in New Haven' (1950), Stevens writes: 'We are not men of bronze and we are not dead.'[24] In another poem, 'Notes Toward A Supreme Fiction' (1942), he imagines a statue of the French general Du Puy as 'a bit absurd', a frozen irrelevancy. Other deaths are recognized by funerals and burials, yet the statue of Du Puy 'Rested immobile', the 'uplifted foreleg of the horse' suspended, as if 'The music halted and the horse stood still'. Whatever Du Puy might have been, the effigy becomes an irrelevant object of idle weekend curiosity, a bourgeois distraction that lawyers or doctors approach in order 'To study the past'. He is not really a person but merely an ornament, 'a setting for geraniums'. The general, the 'very Place Du Puy, in fact, belonged / Among our most vestigial states of mind'. In this atrophied state,

LANDSCAPE AS WEAPON

'Nothing had happened because nothing had changed. / Yet the General was rubbish in the end.'[25]

To avoid being rubbish, change is necessary. Change is the core of Stevens's poetics, and change is a function of the imagination. In other words, statues, because they are designed explicitly not to change, will always be rubbish in the end. They are aesthetically rubbish, second rate, kitsch. And they are rubbish because the times will outgrow them and render them irrelevant garbage. Frank O'Hara, always capable of getting to the point quicker than Stevens, grasped something of the chill in the presence of the frozen effigy, and the need for intimacy as a retort to that coldness, when he wrote, in 'Having A Coke With You' (1960), that 'it is hard to believe when I'm with you that there can be anything as still / as solemn as unpleasantly definitive as statuary when right in front of it'.[26] It is precisely because of their insistence on being 'unpleasantly definitive' that statues have to go.

Statues fail to adapt to circumstances; indeed, lack of adaptability is an aspect of their authority and a big part of the way they embody the sticky hauteur of patriarchy and empire. The authenticity claims of the realist statue, though, are easily open to charges of fakery, as was the case of the iconic Marine Corps War Memorial, commonly known as the Iwo Jima Memorial, in Arlington, Virginia, across the Potomac River from Washington, DC. Depicting the famous flag raising on Iwo Jima during the Second World War and dedicated to all marines who have given their lives since 1775, the photograph upon which the memorial is based is now widely known to have been staged. The danger of authenticity sliding into kitsch is never far away, and sometimes appears despite itself. The inability of many to grasp the austere horizontality of Maya Lin's Vietnam Memorial Wall in Washington, DC, which was dedicated in 1982, led to a compromise commission:

Frederick Hart, once an apprentice to the designer of the Iwo Jima memorial, was invited to produce a bronze figurative sculpture to stand alongside Lin's wall. Hart's *The Three Soldiers*, depicting a white, a Hispanic and an African American serviceman, was unveiled in 1984. The battle-weary figures seem to be looking towards the wall, though the sculpture was initially intended to portray soldiers staring out into the distance. Subsequent memorials installed on the National Mall, including a Women's Memorial (1993) dedicated to those who served in Vietnam, a Korean War Veterans Memorial (1995) and a Second World War memorial (2004), are unlikely to be the last.

Part of the Reverberation of a Windy Night

For Stevens, ordinary public spaces where individuals gather into collective experience might have the capacity to eliminate the overbearing presence of the official monument. In 'An Ordinary Evening in New Haven', 'the marble statues / Are like newspapers blown by the wind.'[27] In that poem a statue of Jove is blown up 'among the boomy clouds', and this iconoclasm is for Stevens, I think, a rejection of the resistance to change embedded in the enshrined and immovable objects that would stand as the monuments to civilization.

Stevens needs to think about statues because of the ways in which they fail as art. Statues are instructive for Stevens, revealing something about the national character despite themselves. A similar spirit, I think, animates another project, this time from the bowels of America's post-Watergate self-examination but which somehow catches the Trump-era spirit of the times. In 2017 the New York-based Eakins Press published a new edition of the influential American street photographer Lee Friedlander's acclaimed 1976 book *The American Monument*, which gathers 213 photographs of urns, obelisks, columns, plaques, pyramids, Neoclassical statuary, birds, horses, generals, soldiers and Native Americans from across the United States. It is an apposite moment for a resurrection of this work, though the new afterword, by Museum of Modern Art photography curator Peter Galassi, does not mention the contemporary culture wars. The focus is on stylistic matters; even the fact that the original volume was published during the American Bicentennial year is considered a coincidence. Nevertheless, *The American Monument* is deeply political in its attentiveness to the contradictions of American memorial culture and the work exudes a sombre, and sometimes sardonic, mood of quiet alienation and declension. The finely printed black and white compositions rarely include people and the monument that is the ostensible subject of the image is not always in the middle of the picture. Indeed, Friedlander's famous off-kilter modernist compositional design sense makes full use of the vernacular environment within which many of the statues appear, and they often struggle for position among street furniture, traffic, foliage, rubbish and other everyday stuff that happens to be in the frame. Similarly, the frame is frequently broken up and divided by vertical blocks of trees or buildings, or by horizontal strips of telephone line. Compressed depth of field creates a jostling of shapes and tones within which the bust or figure or plinth is simply one form among many. Sometimes the statue is almost ridiculously far away, a small silhouette waving or posed heroically and pointlessly in an empty theatre of sky and winter trees.

The cumulative effect is to shrink the monument back into its environment, to make it part of the everyday. As such, Friedlander refuses the role of the monument as the definer of space even as the organizing principle of the collection is that they feature monuments. With so many photographs, and sometimes with six images on a single page, the seriality of the images overrides the specificity of any given monument. The effect flattens significance and the impression becomes one of the American landscape as riddled with what increasingly appears to be an endless sequence of fairly generic markers and effigies. There are lots of firemen and First World War doughboys, a cluster of Native Americans but only two African Americans: statues of W. C. Handy in Memphis, Tennessee, and Bill 'Bojangles' Robinson, in Richmond, Virginia. Civil War monuments are the most common.

A short essay written for the 1976 publication by Leslie George Katz, the founder of Eakins Press, accompanies the photographs. Katz emphasizes the modesty of most of the monuments, each 'a prayer to civil history'.[28] Increasingly impinged upon in an environment 'dominated by menacing speed, instability, advertising and television', the American monument, for Katz, 'plays a meditative role'. There is a 'grace of intention' that 'shines through the ofttimes awkward alliance of efforts that produced them'. This quiet dignity is, he claims, to be found in 'the midst of life', and a public memorial, like a curbstone, 'is a gutter of civic memory, collecting run-offs of communal pride'. At the same time, the awkwardness Katz notes is never far away, since he acknowledges the irony that Americans 'naively memorialize exactly what they have destroyed'. He also sees the humour in many of the images: 'Admittedly tragic now, America is also probably the funniest country in the world.'[29]

The slightly unsteady tone of Katz's essay, oscillating between elegy and irony, is perhaps an accurate response to the complicated reading of American memorial space depicted in Friedlander's images. This is a decidedly Bicentennial view, one that reflects coolly and not uncritically on the traces of America's spatial self-representation. It is a state of the nation assessment, one that enters the culture in the aftermath of Vietnam, Watergate and the oil shocks, and during that brief moment of deflationary self-assessment encouraged by President Jimmy Carter. Like so much of the 'social landscape' photography of the 1960s and many of the so-called New Hollywood films of the early 1970s, *The American Monument* is anti-heroic, lyrical and melancholy, full of empty space and a commitment to street-level formalism. Such an austere and reflexive take on memorial space is in many ways out of place in the angry, polarized twenty-first century. Yet in its capacity to deflate the bellicosity and privilege of the American monument, the Friedlander project remains, in its way, iconoclastic and relevant.

The cumulative effect of *The American Monument* is to give the impression that statues and markers are everywhere, and that effigies of the dead surround us. It may be the absence of people in the photographs, but what Friedlander's project delivers is a weird science-fiction vision of spaces of habitation that could have been built mainly as context for the statues. By gathering together images of so many memorials, Friedlander refuses Musil's claim that in their apparent permanence and part of the lived environment, statues become invisible. A similar sense of insistent visibility is achieved in John Gianvito's 58-minute film *Profit Motive and the Whispering Wind* (2007), which explores the graves and markers across the United States that, inspired by Howard Zinn's *A People's History of the United States, 1492–Present*, memorialize progressive and radical figures and events. As with Friedlander's photographs, there is little contextualizing information given, though the shots of graves, statues and plaques are long enough to allow their contents to be read. Interspersed with the markers are landscape shots, often of a gentle wind moving the trees and grass. This whispering wind, like some spirit of radical history passing across the frame, binds together the celebrated and the little known. The profit motive is the spirit of capitalism against which the tradition of resistance memorialized here pushes. The violence of the struggle and the brutality of the suppression of dissent can only be inferred from the brief descriptive accounts sometimes placed on site. Otherwise, there is only the wind, gently animating the surroundings but revealing little.

Among the graves and memorials collected are those to Anne Hutchinson, Thomas Paine, John Brown, Henry David Thoreau, Chief Crazy Horse, Frederick Douglass, Susan B. Anthony, Harriet Tubman, Eugene Debs, Mother Jones, Emma Goldman, Medgar Evers, Lorraine Hansberry, Malcolm X, John Dos Passos, Paul Goodman, Paul Robeson, Upton Sinclair and Fannie Lou Hamer. Also included are plaques commemorating the slaughter of Native Americans, slave uprisings and the massacre of striking workers. A full list of sites is given in the end credits. Jean-Marie Straub and Danièle Huillet's landscape films, which combine reflections on landscape and past political struggles, are clearly an inspiration, as are the quiet, contemplative films of James Benning.

Zinn's celebrated people's history is intended as a corrective to the distortions of the official American national narrative. As he writes in the afterword, 'Behind every fact presented to the world ... is a judgment. The judgment that has been made is that this fact is important, and that other facts, omitted, are not important.'[30] Zinn's resistance to the 'national interest', a euphemism he sees as an 'all-encompassing veil' that screens off and obscures issues of class, race and gender, produces a counter-narrative that imagines a permanent and persistent collective spirit of defiance. By focusing on the graves and memorials, while Gianvito risks establishing a context only for mourning, he also exposes a long history of memorialization at odds with the domination of space that characterizes so many monuments to causes perceived to be won or lost. The memorials in Gianvito's film are not objective markers of an uncontested history. Rather, they are markers of contestation. While often the statues appear similar in form to the triumphant or tragic monuments erected by advocates of nation, section or caste, their presence complicates the reading of monuments as, by definition, acts of domination.

A Wild Card in the World of Politics

The removal of monuments to white supremacy in the United States suggests that the inventory of counter-monuments to a people's history is not enough. Stevens's insistent iconoclasm seems more fitting as it recognizes the very presence of the statue as the defiant embodiment of a refusal to change. The statue's claim to permanence is exactly what must be defied. During the American Revolution, the Sons of Liberty pulled down and destroyed the gilt lead statue of George III on Bowling Green, New York City, melting it down for use as musket balls against the British Army. The surge of popular resistance to dictators often quickly leads to the downing of symbolic figures. The Hungarian uprising in 1956 saw Stalin toppled in Budapest, a dry run for the waves of statue destruction at the end of the Cold War. Lenin, Stalin and Marx all fell, becoming indicative not only of the end of oppressive regimes but of the triumph of the West. In these instances, as in the much photographed toppling of the statue of Saddam Hussein in Iraq in 2003, the destruction of monuments is achieved in the name of democracy, and as a demonstration of the temporary reality of what had claimed to be permanent.

Iconoclasm, though, can move in the other direction, seeking to impose new realities by permanently destroying history. For example, when the Taliban destroyed two ancient statues of Buddha at Bamyan in Afghanistan in 2005, it was seen as vandalism. Destroying monuments makes new claims on time as well as space.

Curiously, the act of iconoclasm itself also often seeks a memorial, and in some parts of Europe and in Russia the fallen statues of communism are being returned as reminders of the overthrow of repressive regimes. In Budapest, Memento Park, containing dozens of communist-era statues, opened as early as 1993, two years to the day after the withdrawal of Russian troops. In 2015, the head of a giant Lenin monument famously chopped up and buried in Berlin in 1991 was excavated and installed as part of an exhibition called 'Unveiled: Berlin and its Monuments' at the Spandau Citadel that included communist and Nazi statues as well as older monuments to Prussian militarism. These shifts and reappraisals are not really new and repeat the endless adjustments made through history to the order and prominence of statues and monuments, suggesting that Stevens's will to change is to be found less in the objects themselves but in the turbulent and endless reinscription of meaning. As Michael North writes:

> The entire assembled sculpture collection of the Western world was subject to . . . dislocation of identity in the eighteenth and nineteenth centuries, when Roman names were removed under the influence of Winckelmann's idea that the great statues were Greek works, and then again when modern scholarship established that they were probably Roman copies after all. Some of these shifts are certainly trivial, but there is something about a statue and

its combination of didactic power with a certain inevitable generality of reference that makes it a kind of wild card in the world of politics.[31]

This wild-card quality sometimes leads to some unexpected responses, especially when the signs of oppression themselves become the objects of a curious mode of longing.

'It may seem only right', Laura Mulvey writes, reflecting on the investigations she and Mark Lewis conducted in the former Soviet Union for their film *Disgraced Monuments* (1994), 'to wipe out the triumphalist remnants of a fascist regime, especially when a people suddenly finds itself able to impose a collective, symbolic vengeance on these objects and especially when their aesthetic value reflects their political significance.' Yet there are broader matters to be considered, she goes on, relating to memory and repression within history: 'The monuments erected by a hated regime may also, after its fall, perform an emblematic function in reverse.'[32]

In their investigation of the iconoclasm following the collapse of communism, problematically, Mulvey and Lewis discovered that, for many, the removal of statues at the end of the Soviet Union recalled the iconoclasm that the communists had themselves instigated seventy years earlier when they removed monuments to the Tsars. Over and over, Mulvey writes, 'people connected the latest wave of iconoclasm with Lenin's own first removal of Tsarist statues and religious icons', to the point where it seemed that Lenin's iconoclastic decree lived on even as monuments to Lenin disappeared. Many of the people Mulvey and Lewis interviewed in 1991 said that 'an ability to live with monuments to the heroes of communism would now mark an ability to live with the past, however hostile to that past they might be personally.'[33]

The claim here that ultimately living with the monuments is better than destroying them is by no means an uncomplicated or even reconciliatory one. In the context of, say, the ongoing challenges to the presence of monuments to Confederate warriors, the notion of learning to live with monuments sounds too close to what communities have been doing all along throughout the Southern states.

Yet Mark Lewis's argument about making visible the monument's claim to authority might enable a challenge that does not necessarily lead to literal destruction. Indeed, without a transfiguration of the monument's symbolic power and the conditions under which that power was held in place, the destruction of the monument is unlikely, in itself, to change very much. The kind of critical cultural work that Lewis proposes does not exclude the possibility of demolition, but it also introduces the deflationary possibilities of the toppled, defaced or ruined monument as itself a memorial to history. The public work, Lewis writes, serves two ends and one 'ultimately undermines the other':

> The monument covers up the crimes against the public in so far as it is able to temporarily 'smother' the possibility of remembering specific histories in terms of the violence that engendered them; instead, it commemorates a history or event in terms of a pernicious heroism or nationalism. At the same time, the monument exists as a perpetual marker, a reminder of those very crimes. It waves a red flag, so to speak, on the site of its repressions. And when the symbolic order is thrown into crisis, the public monument's semantic charge shifts and the work becomes less heroic in form but rather begins to take on the characteristics of a scar.[34]

It is the disgrace of the monument that can allow for a change of meaning that does not deny the original claims made by the monument but overwrites them. 'Once disgraced', Mulvey explains, 'the passing of time can shift the monument's meaning further, out of the political into emotional or cultural resonance. Many people have noted that fallen statues can acquire a certain kind of pathos.'[35] Referring to felled Soviet monuments, Mulvey describes them 'lying incongruously and ignominiously on the ground', without dignity 'as children play on them', their 'very scale underlines their helplessness'. Eventually they might 'acquire a curiosity value', 'find a demand abroad' or, abandoned and moss-covered, 'take on something of the romance of ruins and the mysteriousness of Ozymandias'.[36] This is Musil's indifference, weaponized.

Conclusion

Practices of accumulation, gathering together, collecting and cataloguing, preservation and display, characterize much of the work discussed in this book. Hoarding and the curatorial spirit are obviously central to Mike Nelson's *The Asset Strippers*, but the drive to collect is also there in Ronald Blythe's transcription of oral histories and Robert Macfarlane's glossaries; in the proliferation of photographic dereliction known as ruin porn; in projects by artists, heritage professionals and enthusiasts to explore and classify old military sites; and in the work on monuments by Lee Friedlander and John Gianvito. Many of the photographic projects and films discussed here rely on strategies of seriality, repetition and difference that can only be achieved through the stacking and arrangement of gathered materials. They are rarely concerned with the singular instance and more often than not preoccupied with the relations among the parts. This, I think, is also true of Macfarlane, Iain Sinclair and other non-fiction writers for whom the coherence of narrative relies upon the threading together of scraps of information and experience into an arrangement that sometimes looks like order. The attraction of following old pathways or the M25 provides a coherence that defines and gives pace to the episodic. The process is, as in Sinclair's proliferating clauses, cumulative.

This preoccupation with the collection and arrangement of things is, in many cases, about spatializing time, though in different ways. There is, on the one hand, a powerful preservationist impulse at work in many of the works considered here. Voices must be recorded, idioms must be remembered, places and species must be saved, stories must not be forgotten. While there is often a profound, sometimes palpable sense of loss permeating much of this work, the necessity for preservation is rarely, at least intentionally, about the erection of shrines to the lost. Instead, in many cases what is driving the examination of remains and remnants is a commitment to the reactivation or reanimation of dormant (or even dead) powers. On the other hand, the domination of contemporary space by past times has also become increasingly apparent, and here a countervailing push to refuse the authority of historical legacies is precisely aimed at resisting preservation. Statues must come down, secrets must be revealed, structural inequalities must be dug out.

The preservationists and iconoclasts are not necessarily different constituencies, since what is at stake here is not simply a contest between conservatives and progressives, as if past and future, persistence and change could be neatly positioned on the political spectrum. The practices of accumulation and curatorial arrangement that have come to characterize so much of contemporary culture in advanced capitalist countries are, at once, I think, both modes of acquiescence and resistance. They are responses to a culture geared towards overconsumption and a normalized rhetoric of creative destruction, but they are radically contested practices that are never straightforwardly regenerative or destructive. Who gets to choose what is collected and what is discarded? Who gets to say that this strip of toxic scrubland is, in fact, a site for emancipatory thinking? Why should it be desirable for the wrecked fortifications of totalitarian regimes to be retooled as items on a tourist itinerary? Only those willing to speak get their stories transcribed, and only those structures that speak to some deeply encoded vocabulary of taste get to be called ruins.

The controversies over statues of racists are instructive here and may well mark a shift away from the curatorial, archival, memorial sensibility that has emerged and flourished since the 1970s. Mid-twentieth-century poets such as Wallace Stevens rejected heroic statuary as kitsch and irrelevant to the protean spirit of modernity. Contemporary distaste for old statues, though, is rarely expressed in aesthetic terms: it is the perpetuation of institutionalized racism, physically occupying and continuing to dominate public space, not the poor quality of the composition, that is at issue. Stevens does not mention Andrew Jackson's record as a slave owner and killer of Native Americans when he challenges the statue in Lafayette Square, but these are now precisely the reasons given in calls for such monuments to be removed. What is unambiguous in relation to the status of statues is that the past is not over.

Despite the argument that education can best and most properly reposition the meaning of offending statuary, and that getting rid of the things will merely vandalize historic spaces, only the physical act of removal (and the circulation of images of them being so removed) seems to truly and satisfactorily mark the rejection of the values enshrined there. For different reasons, perhaps, both Henry James and Wallace Stevens would probably have had Sherman and Jackson melted down if they could. Laura Mulvey and Mark Lewis warned, in the early 1990s, of the danger of eradicating statues of hated figures, since their demolition threatened to erase evidence that they ever existed, thereby denying the reality of the suffering they caused. Contemporary

LANDSCAPE AS WEAPON

debates over statues of imperialists and racists, by contrast, show little concern that eliminating monuments to tyranny and hatred will ultimately lead to the repression of facts. What is compelling in the case of racist statues is the willingness by those opposed to them to reject both the heritage and the repression defence. Someone might wish to make a collection of these disgraced monuments, like they did in the old Eastern Bloc, but they are unlikely to survive in their present locations.

The issue here, it seems to me, in the context of the broader issues explored in this book, turns on the economy of preservation and destruction. Imagine, for a moment, that the approach to racist statues was applied to other categories of redundant or worn-out things and places. Perhaps the beaches should be cleared of Hitler's noxious concrete defences, however much they look like crashed Martian spacecraft. Instead of eulogizing the contaminated edgelands as magical middle landscapes operating as portals between the country and the city, what would happen if the deformations of space by the real estate business were seriously challenged? What if we accepted that the fields of England worked as a screen memory to conceal the fact that generations of labourers were worked to death upon them?

The statue removals are compelling because they provide a bracing alternative to what has become, as we have seen, a culture in thrall to the legacies of the past, either as an inescapable burden of brutality and suffering or as an irretrievably lost domain of security and authenticity. My point here is not necessarily to advocate bunker demolition or the end to edgeland reverie, any more than I am suggesting that the removal of offensive old statues marks an end to the racist oppression they represent. The danger, however, is that the curatorial and archival strategies of accumulation and preservation seen at work throughout these pages, practices often claimed as counter-hegemonic and operating at the margins of official discourse, have become the conventional spaces of neutralized dissent: the canonization of Ballard, a coffee-table book of Detroit ruins, a day trip to Orford Ness, and a wander round *The Asset Strippers* at the Tate.

As I suggested in the context of so-called ruin porn, the sheer volume of similar images can serve to rinse out criticality. Complex histories become flattened into a series of familiar tropes and tics, the process of accumulation itself operating as a mode of decontextualizing violence that privileges similarities over differences. The typological tendencies of a visual culture interested in stockpiling images of bunkers or derelict houses or monuments or factories will require a particular mode of attention in order to prevent those typologies becoming generalities. Perhaps the flattening is itself the point, a kind of Warholian degradation of particularity. More promising, I think, is the insistence, among some of the works encountered here, on the long look, the delayed response, the reflexive gesture, the slow reckoning. Admittedly, this can sometimes turn into another mode of connoisseurship, whereby only the properly attuned and time rich can hope to grasp what is going on. On the other hand, if the last five decades or so have generated a culture dedicated to coming to terms with the acceleration of destruction, it is partly because the preservationist impulse demands of its objects a longer period of contemplation.

In her recent book *Learning from the Germans*, philosopher Susan Neiman argues that if the United States is to seriously approach the legacy of its racist past it must be prepared to undertake the long, difficult and endless work Germany found it necessary to begin after the Second World War. With reference also to the history of British imperialism, Neiman quotes the former British Museum director Neil MacGregor, who noted in 2015 that while the Germans use their past to think about the future, 'the British tend to use their history to comfort themselves'.[1] What is disturbing about the tendency on the Right, intensified and emboldened by the events of 2016 in the u.s. and the UK, to insist upon a falsified version of the national past as a lost utopia is that this version of history is currently serving less as a comfort and more as a model for the future.

Works like *The Asset Strippers* may come to be seen as the end of a cultural wave, the end of a culture fixated on endings, depletions and redundancies. As the climate crisis intensifies, though, it is unlikely that we are done with narratives of exhaustion just yet. The best of the work discussed here, I think, manages, nevertheless, to refuse exhaustion even when that condition is the ostensible subject. The removal of statues suggests that there are other moves yet to be made and that what appears to be permanent can nevertheless, one day, be made to go away.

REFERENCES

Introduction

1 Laura Cumming, 'Mike Nelson: The Asset Strippers Review –
  His All-time Masterpiece', *The Observer*, www.theguardian.com,
  24 March 2019.
2 Charles Baudelaire, 'Du vin et du haschisch' (1851), cited in Walter
  Benjamin, *The Arcades Project*, trans. Howard Eiland (Cambridge,
  MA, 2002), p. 349. On Benjamin's use of Baudelaire's figure of
  the ragpicker as a model for the materialist historian, see Irving
  Wohlfarth, 'Et Cetera? The Historian as Chiffonnier', *New German
  Critique*, XXXIX (1986), pp. 142–68. For a sympathetic and self-
  reflexive cinematic meditation on scavenging as a mode of survival
  and of art, see Agnès Varda, *Les Glaneurs et la glaneuse* (2000).
3 The science-fiction dimension is not accidental. Nelson cites
  Roadside Picnic, the cult 1972 Russian novel written by Arkady
  and Boris Strugatsky, as an influence. The source text for Andrei
  Tarkovsky's *Stalker* (1979), *Roadside Picnic* imagines how the
  rubbish left behind by an alien visitation becomes a source of fear
  and fascination.
4 Don Mitchell, 'Dead Labor and the Political Economy of
  Landscape – California Living, California Dying', in *Handbook of
  Cultural Geography*, ed. Kay Anderson, Mona Domosh, Steve Pile
  and Nigel Thrift (London, 2003), pp. 233–48, p. 241.
5 W.J.T. Mitchell, 'Introduction', in *Landscape and Power*, ed. W.J.T.
  Mitchell (Chicago, IL, 1994), pp. 1–4, p. 1.
6 On memory, see Andreas Huyssen, 'Present Pasts: Media, Politics,
  Amnesia', *Public Culture*, XII/1 (2000), pp. 21–38.
7 For Derrida's use of hauntology, see Jacques Derrida, *Spectres of
  Marx*: *The State of the Debt, the Work of Mourning, and the New
  International,* trans. Peggy Kamuf (New York, 1994). For the
  subsequent critical debate, see Michael Sprinker, ed., *Ghostly
  Demarcations: A Symposium on Jacques Derrida's Specters of Marx*

(London, 1999); Roger Luckhurst, 'The Contemporary London Gothic and the Limits of the "Spectral Turn"', *Textual Practice*, XVI/3 (2002), pp. 527–47; Mark Fisher, 'What Is Hauntology?', *Film Quarterly*, LXVI/1 (2012), pp. 16–24. For discussion of the hauntological in relation to music, see, for example, Mark Fisher, *Ghosts of My Life: Writings on Depression, Hauntology and Lost Futures* (Winchester, 2014) and Simon Reynolds, *Retromania: Pop Culture's Addiction to Its Own Past* (London, 2011). On the persistence of a British folk tradition, in all its weird manifestations, see Rob Young, *Electric Eden: Unearthing Britain's Visionary Music* (London, 2010).

8 On the problem of nostalgia for the Left, see Alastair Bonnett, 'The Dilemmas of Radical Nostalgia in British Psychogeography', *Theory, Culture and Society*, XXVI/1 (2009), pp. 45–70; Alastair Bonnett, *Left in the Past: Radicalism and the Politics of Nostalgia* (London, 2010). Owen Hatherley is good on situating austerity nostalgia within a broader context of national identity in *The Ministry of Nostalgia: Consuming Austerity* (London, 2016).

9 Ernst Bloch, *Heritage of Our Times*, trans. Neville and Stephen Plaice (Cambridge, 1991). See also Ernst Bloch, 'Nonsynchronism and the Obligation to Its Dialectics', trans. Mark Ritter, *New German Critique*, XI (1977), pp. 22–38; Anson Rabinbach, 'Unclaimed Heritage: Ernst Bloch's Heritage of Our Times and the Theory of Fascism', *New German Critique*, XI (1977), pp. 5–21; Frederic J. Schwartz, 'Ernst Bloch and Wilhelm Pinder: Out of Sync', *Grey Room*, III (2001), pp. 54–89.

10 Hans Ulrich Gumbrecht, *After 1945: Latency as Origin of the Present* (Stanford, CA, 2013), pp. 22–3.

11 Ibid., p. 28.

12 Ibid., pp. 199–200.

13 Mike Nelson quoted in Hettie Judah, 'Fire Sale Britain: Mike Nelson on Why He Turned the Tate into a Big Salvage Yard', *The Guardian*, www.theguardian.com, 18 March 2019.

1 What Will Become of England?

1 On Harry Cox, see Peter Kennedy, Harry Cox and Francis Collinson, 'Harry Cox: English Folk Singer', *Journal of the English Folk Dance and Song Society*, XIII/3 (1958), pp. 142–55.

2 Martin Ryle, 'After "Organic Community": Ecocriticism, Nature, and Human Nature', in *The Environmental Tradition in English Literature*, ed. John Parham (Aldershot, 2002), pp. 11–14, p. 22; Raymond Williams, *The Country and the City* (Oxford, 1973), pp. 9–12.

3 David Matless, *Landscape and Englishness* (London, 1998), pp. 16–17.

4 On folk revivals and the idea of an authentic cultural past, see, for example, Georgina Boyes, *The Imagined Village: Culture, Ideology and the English Folk Revival*, revd ed. (Leeds, 2010); Michael Brocken, *The British Folk Revival, 1944–2002* (Aldershot, 2003).

5 Ronald Blythe, *Akenfield: Portrait of an English Village* (London, 2005).

6 Raphael Samuel, 'Perils of the Transcript' (1971), in *The Oral History Reader*, ed. Robert Perks and Alistair Thomson (London, 1998), pp. 389–92, p. 389.

7 Ibid., p. 389.

8 Ibid., p. 391. On Evans, see Alun Howkins, 'Inventing Everyman: George Ewart Evans, Oral History and National Identity', *Oral History*, xxv (1994), pp. 26–32.

9 Jan Marsh, 'Review: A Miraculous Relic?', *Cambridge Quarterly*, vi/1 (1972), pp. 70–77, p. 72.

10 Ibid., p. 72.

11 Ibid., p. 73.

12 Ibid., p. 76.

13 Howard Newby, 'Akenfield Revisited', *Oral History*, iii/1 (1975), pp. 76–83, p. 78.

14 Ibid., p. 78.

15 Ibid., p. 79.

16 Ibid.

17 Ibid., p. 80.

18 Ibid.

19 Paul Thompson, *The Voice of the Past: Oral History*, 3rd edn (Oxford, 2000), p. 102.

20 Ibid., p. 102.

21 See Lynn Abrams, *Oral History Theory* (Abingdon, 2010), pp. 5–7.

22 On the 'new nature writing', see Joe Moran, 'A Cultural History of the New Nature Writing', *Literature and History*, xxiii/1 (2014), pp. 49–63.

23 Blythe, *Akenfield*, p. 8.

24 Ibid.

25 Newby, 'Akenfield Revisited', p. 81.

26 Blythe, *Akenfield*, p. 10.

27 Kathleen Jamie, 'A Lone Enraptured Male: Review: The Wild Places by Robert Macfarlane', *London Review of Books*, xxx/5 (6 March 2008), pp. 25–7.

28 Mark Cocker, 'Death of the Naturalist: Why Is the "New Nature Writing" So Tame?', *New Statesman*, www.newstatesman.com, 17 June 2015.

29 Ibid.

30 Newby, 'Akenfield Revisited', p. 76.

31 Robert Macfarlane, 'Ghost Species', *Granta*, CII, The New Nature Writing (2008), pp. 109–28, p. 109.
32 Robert Macfarlane, *Landmarks* (London, 2015), p. 2.
33 In their illustrated book for children, *The Lost Words* (London, 2017), Macfarlane and artist Jackie Morris defiantly reclaimed the expunged nature words from the *Oxford Junior Dictionary*.
34 Macfarlane, *Landmarks*, p. 4.
35 Ibid., p. 14.
36 Ibid., p. 10.
37 Peter Hall, quoted in Paul Newland, *British Films of the 1970s* (Manchester, 2015), p. 151.
38 Newby, 'Akenfield Revisited', pp. 80–82.
39 Blythe, *Akenfield*, pp. 38–9.
40 Ibid., p. 99.
41 Ibid.
42 Ibid., p. 239.
43 Ibid., p. 54.
44 Ibid., p. 68.
45 Raphael Samuel, *Theatres of Memory: Past and Present in Contemporary Culture* (London, 1994), vol. I, p. 197.
46 John C. Tibbetts, 'Kevin Brownlow's Historical Films: *It Happened Here* (1965) and *Winstanley* (1975)', *Historical Journal of Film, Radio and Television*, XX/2 (2000), pp. 227–51, p. 251.
47 Nicholas J. Cull, 'Peter Watkins' *Culloden* and the Alternative Form in Historical Filmmaking', in *Retrovisions: Reinventing the Past in Film and Fiction*, ed. Deborah Cartmell, I. Q. Hunter and Imelda Whelehan (London, 2001), pp. 87–101, p. 90.
48 Kynan Gentry, '"The Pathos of Conservation": Raphael Samuel and the Politics of Heritage', *International Journal of Heritage Studies*, XXI/6 (2015), pp. 561–76, p. 565.
49 Alex Farquharson, 'Jeremy Deller: The Battle of Orgreave, London, UK', *Frieze*, LXI, https://frieze.com, September 2001.
50 See Alice Correia, 'Interpreting Jeremy Deller's The Battle of Orgreave', *Visual Culture in Britain*, XII/2 (2006), pp. 93–112.
51 See David Gilbert, '*The English Civil War Part II: Personal Accounts of the 1984–85 Miners' Strike* by Jeremy Deller', *Oral History*, XXXI/1 (2005), pp. 104–5. For an oral history of the miners' strike from the 1980s, see Raphael Samuel, Barbara Bloomfield and Guy Boanas, eds, *The Enemy Within: Pit Villages and the Miners' Strike of 1984–5* (London, 1986).

2 Dreary Secrets of the Universe

1 Robert Smithson, 'A Tour of the Monuments of Passaic, New Jersey (1967)', in *Robert Smithson: The Collected Writings*, ed. Jack Flam (Berkeley, CA, 1996), pp. 68–74, pp. 68, 69.
2 Ibid., p. 74.
3 Ibid., p. 69.
4 Ann Reynolds, *Robert Smithson: Learning from New Jersey and Elsewhere* (Cambridge, MA, 2004), p. 101.
5 Smithson, 'A Tour of the Monuments of Passaic', pp. 71, 72.
6 Ibid., pp. 73–4.
7 Ibid., p. 71.
8 Ignasi de Solà-Morales, 'Terrain Vague', in *Anyplace*, ed. Cynthia C. Davidson (Cambridge, MA, 1995), pp. 118–23, pp. 119–20.
9 Ibid., p. 120.
10 Alan Berger, *Drosscape: Wasting Land in Urban America* (Princeton, NJ, 2006), p. 12.
11 Marion Shoard, 'Edgelands', in *Remaking the Landscape: The Changing Face of Britain*, ed. Jennifer Jenkins (London, 2002), pp. 117–46, p. 117.
12 Ibid., p. 141.
13 Paul Farley and Michael Symmons Roberts, *Edgelands: Journeys into England's True Wilderness* (London, 2011), p. 14.
14 Solà-Morales, 'Terrain Vague', pp. 122–3.
15 Ibid., p. 123.
16 Allen Ginsberg, 'Sunflower Sutra', in *Collected Poems, 1947–1997* (New York, 2007), p. 147.
17 Robert Macfarlane, 'A Road of One's Own: Past and Present Artists of the Randomly Motivated Walk', *Times Literary Supplement* (7 October 2005), pp. 3–4, p. 4.
18 John Heartfield, 'Londonostalgia', www.heartfield.org, accessed 1 November 2019.
19 See David James, *Contemporary British Fiction and the Artistry of Space: Style, Landscape, Perception* (London, 2009), pp. 85–6. 'The temptation, as always, stood firm', writes Sinclair, 'to inflate a day's wandering, out in the weather, into something that could be described as a "quest."' Iain Sinclair, *Lights Out for the Territory: 9 Excursions in the Secret History of London* (London, 1997), p. 113.
20 Iain Sinclair, *London Orbital: A Walk Around the M25* (London, 2002), p. 11.
21 Joe Moran, *Reading the Everyday* (Abingdon, 2005), p. 98.
22 Sinclair, *London Orbital*, p. 397.
23 This sense of the wild being near-at-hand is a preoccupation of much edgelands writing, most extensively developed by one

of the godfathers of the new nature writing, Richard Mabey, in his influential 1973 book *The Unofficial Countryside* (Wimborne Minster, 2010), and more recently in *Weeds: How Vagabond Plants Gatecrashed Civilisation and Changed the Way We Think About Nature* (London, 2010).

24 Jon Savage, 'The Things That Aren't There Anymore', *Critical Quarterly*, I/1–2 (2008), pp. 180–97, p. 181.
25 Ibid., p. 183.
26 Jon Savage, *England's Dreaming: The Sex Pistols and Punk Rock* (London, 2005), p. 112.
27 Dick Hebdige, *Subculture: The Meaning of Style* (London, 1979), p. 24.
28 Savage, 'Things', pp. 193–4.
29 Savage, *England's Dreaming*, p. 136.
30 Deborah Curtis quoted in Savage, 'Things', p. 191.
31 Ibid., pp. 194–5.
32 The Thames Estuary and the ragged fringes of Essex are no strangers to edgeland writers and photographers. See, for example, the two sharply focused books produced by writer Ken Worpole and photographer Jason Orton, *350 Miles: An Essex Journey* (Colchester, 2005) and *The New English Landscape* (London, 2013). Robert Macfarlane made a BBC documentary in 2009 called *The Wild Places of Essex*, and Rachel Lichtenstein's *Estuary: Out from London to the Sea* (London, 2016) soaks up the atmosphere.
33 Laura Oldfield Ford, *Savage Messiah* (London, 2011).
34 For a wider range of anti-Olympic art and culture, see Hillary Powell and Isaac Marrero-Guillamón, *The Art of Dissent: Adventures in London's Olympic State* (London, 2012).

3 The Poverty of Ruins

1 John Hillcoat quoted in Tom Chiarella, 'The Most Important Movie of the Year', *Esquire* (June 2009), pp. 87–91, p. 91.
2 On urban exploration, see David Pinder, 'Arts of Urban Exploration', *Cultural Geographies*, XII (2005), pp. 383–411; Bradley Garrett, *Explore Everything: Place-hacking the City* (London, 2013); Sylvain Margaine, *Forbidden Places: Exploring our Abandoned Heritage* (Versailles, 2009); Ninjalicious, *Access All Areas: A User's Guide to the Art of Urban Exploration* (Toronto, 2005).
3 On rubble, see Jeff Byles, *Rubble: Unearthing the History of Demolition* (New York, 2005); Gastón Gordillo, *Rubble: The Afterlife of Destruction* (Durham, NC, 2014).
4 On ruins, see Rose Macaulay, *Pleasure of Ruins* (London, 1953); Paul Zucker, *Fascination of Decay: Ruins: Relic – Symbol*

– *Ornament* (Ridgewood, NJ, 1968). For an American context, see Nick Yablon, *Untimely Ruins: An Archaeology of American Urban Modernity, 1819–1919* (Chicago, IL, 2009).

5 Andreas Huyssen, *Twilight Memories: Marking Time in a Culture of Amnesia* (New York, 1995); Julia Hell and Andreas Schönle, eds, *Ruins of Modernity* (Durham, NC, 2010).

6 On the aftermath of the Second World War, see, for example, James E. Young, 'The Counter-monument: Memory Against itself in Germany Today', *Critical Inquiry*, XVIII/2 (1996), pp. 267–96; Julia Hell, 'Ruins Travel: Orphic Journeys through Germany's Ruins', in *Writing Travel*, ed. John Zilcosky (Baltimore, MD, 2008), pp. 123–60; Jerzy Elzanowski, 'Manufacturing Ruins: Architecture and Representation in Post-catastrophic Warsaw', *Journal of Architecture*, XV/1 (2010), pp. 67–82. On heritage and 'dark tourism', see John Frow, 'Tourism and the Semiotics of Nostalgia', *October*, LVII (1991), pp. 123–51; Elizabeth Diller and Ricardo Scofidio, eds, *Back to the Front: Tourisms of War* (Princeton, NJ, 1996); John Lennon and Malcolm Foley, *Dark Tourism: The Attraction of Death and Disaster* (London, 2000). On China, see Greg Gerard, *Phantom Shanghai* (Toronto, 2010). On the world after 'us', see Alan Weisman, *The World Without Us* (London, 2008) and Jan Zalasiewicz, *The Earth After Us: What Legacy Will Humans Leave in the Rocks?* (Oxford, 2008).

7 Barrett Watten, 'Learning from Detroit: The Poetics of Ruined Space', *Detroit Research*, 1, www.detroitresearch.org (2014).

8 Denis Linehan, 'An Archaeology of Dereliction: Poetics and Policy in the Governing of Depressed Industrial Districts in Interwar England and Wales', *Journal of Historical Geography*, XXVI/1 (2000), pp. 99–113, p. 101.

9 Ibid., p. 101.

10 Ibid.

11 Christopher Woodward, *In Ruins* (London, 2002), p. 139.

12 Tim Edensor, *Industrial Ruins: Spaces, Aesthetics and Materiality* (Oxford, 2005), p. 4.

13 Camilo José Vergara, 'Downtown Detroit: American Acropolis or Vacant Land?', *Metropolis* (April 1995), pp. 33–8, p. 36.

14 Camilo José Vergara, *The New American Ghetto* (New Brunswick, NJ, 1995); *American Ruins* (New York, 1999).

15 U.S. Census Bureau, www.census.gov; World Population Review, www.worldpopulationreview.com, accessed 5 September 2019.

16 Christine MacDonald, 'Suburbs Gain While Detroit Population Drops Below 700,000', *Detroit News*, www.detroitnews.com, 21 May 2014.

17 Bureau of Labor Statistics, Local Area Unemployment Statistics:

Unemployment Rates for the 50 Largest Cities (Based on Census 2000 Population), www.bls.gov, accessed 16 February 2015.

18 Thomas J. Sugrue, *The Origins of the Urban Crisis: Race and Inequality in Postwar Detroit* (Princeton, NJ, 1996), pp. 126, 148.

19 Ibid., p. 155.

20 Dan Austin and Sean Doerr, *Lost Detroit: Stories Behind the Motor City's Majestic Ruins* (Charleston, SC, 2010); Yves Marchand and Romain Meffre, *The Ruins of Detroit* (Göttingen, 2010); Andrew Moore, *Detroit Disassembled* (Bologna and Akron, OH, 2010).

21 See, for example, Holly Brubach, 'Ruin With a View', *New York Times Magazine*, www.nytimes.com, 9 April 2010; Amy Sullivan, 'Postcard from Detroit', *Time*, https://time.com, 30 April 2009; Rebecca Solnit, 'Detroit Arcadia: Exploring the Post-American Landscape', *Harper's Magazine* (July 2007), pp. 65–73; Sean O'Hagan, 'Detroit in Ruins', *The Observer*, www.theguardian.com, 2 January 2011.

22 For more on the cultural responses to the shifting fortunes of Detroit, see Dora Apel, *Beautiful Terrible Ruins: Detroit and the Anxiety of Decline* (New Brunswick, NJ, 2015); Rebecca J. Kinney, *Beautiful Wasteland: The Rise of Detroit as America's Postindustrial Frontier* (Minneapolis, MN, 2016).

23 The text from 'Imaging Detroit' is still available at https://archpapers.com/imaging-detroit-iiii-competition.

24 Watten, 'Learning'.

25 See Kinney, *Beautiful Wasteland*, pp. 38–64.

26 Andrew Herscher, *The Unreal Estate Guide to Detroit* (Ann Arbor, MI, 2012). See also Kimberley Kinder, *DIY Detroit: Making Do in a City Without Services* (Minnesota, MN, 2016); John Gallagher, *Revolution Detroit: Strategies for Urban Reinvention* (Detroit, MI, 2013).

27 Drew Philp, *A $500 House in Detroit: Rebuilding an Abandoned Home and an American City* (New York, 2017).

28 Kinney, *Beautiful Wasteland*, p. 51.

29 Ibid., p. 44.

30 Michael Chanan in George Steinmetz and Michael Chanan, 'Drive-by Shooting: Filming Detroit: Interviews with the Filmmakers' (2005), www.detroitruinofacity.com, accessed 1 November 2019.

31 See Liam Kennedy, *Race and Urban Space in American Culture* (Edinburgh, 2000), pp. 113–14.

32 Steinmetz and Chanan, 'Drive-by Shooting', www.detroitruinofacity.com, accessed 1 November 2019 .

33 Michigan Film Production, www.michiganfilmproduction.com, accessed 16 February 2015.

34 Sharon Silke Carty, 'Michigan Tax Credit Courts Film Industry to Lure Money, Jobs', *USA Today*, https://abcnews.go.com, 17 August 2009.

35 Amy Chozick, 'Motown Becomes Movietown', *Wall Street Journal*, www.online.wsj.com, 17 September 2010.

36 Carty, 'Michigan Tax Credit'.

37 Charlotte Philby, 'Living in Ghostland: The Last Heygate Residents', *The Independent*, www.independent.co.uk, 29 March 2010; Owen Hatherley, 'After the Heygate Estate, A Grey Future Awaits', *The Guardian*, www.guardian.com, 8 February 2011. Estates like the Aylesbury and the Heygate are precisely the kind of buildings Hatherley celebrates in his own expeditions into the lost future of British socialism. See his *Militant Modernism* (London, 2009) and *A Guide to the New Ruins of Great Britain* (London, 2010).

38 On the importance of New York City in creating a cinematic iconography of bankruptcy and decay, see Stanley Corkin, *Starring New York: Filming the Grime and the Glamour of the Long 1970s* (New York, 2011).

39 Anna Minton, 'The Price of Regeneration', *Places*, https://placesjournal.org, September 2018.

40 Bruce Katz and Jeremy Nowak, *The New Localism: How Cities Can Thrive in the Age of Populism* (Washington, DC, 2018), p. 27.

41 Ibid.

42 Quoted in Jillian Steinhauser, 'Finishing "Mobile Homestead" After the Death of the Artist', *Hyperallergic*, https://hyperallergic.com, 17 May 2012.

43 Edensor, *Industrial Ruins*, p. 4.

4 Invisible from Here On In

1 Paul Virilio, *Bunker Archeology*, trans. George Collins (Princeton, NJ, 1994), p. 39.

2 Ibid.

3 W. G. Sebald, *Austerlitz*, trans. Anthea Bell (London, 2002), p. 16.

4 Ibid., p. 25.

5 Ibid., pp. 25–6.

6 Ibid., p. 26.

7 W. G. Sebald, *The Rings of Saturn*, trans. Michael Hulse (London, 1998), p. 237. For more on Suffolk's militarized landscape, see Sophia Davis, *Island Thinking: Suffolk's Stories of Landscape, Militarisation and Identity* (London, 2019).

8 Ibid., p. 236.

9 Robert Macfarlane, *The Wild Places* (London, 2007), p. 257.

10 Sigmund Freud, *Totem and Taboo: Resemblances between the Psychic Lives of Savages and Neurotics*, trans. A. A. Brill (New York, 1919).

11 Zygmunt Bauman, *Modernity and Ambivalence* (Cambridge, 1991), p. 15. Original emphasis.

12 Christopher Woodward, *In Ruins* (London, 2002), p. 224.

13 Sebald, *The Rings of Saturn*, p. 237.

14 For further discussion of Virilio's bunker project, see Mike Gane, 'Paul Virilio's Bunker Theorizing', in *Paul Virilio: From Modernism to Hypermodernism and Beyond*, ed. John Armitage (London, 2000), pp. 85–102.

15 Bernd and Hiller Becher, quoted in *Bernd and Hiller Becher, Typologies*, ed. Armin Zweite (Cambridge, MA, 2004), p. 9.

16 Michael Waterhouse, quoted in Keith Mallory and Arvid Ottar, *Architecture of Aggression: A History of Military Architecture in North West Europe, 1900–1945* (London, 1973), p. 9.

17 Reyner Banham, *A Concrete Atlantis: U.S. Industrial Building and European Modern Architecture, 1900–1925* (Cambridge, MA, 1989), p. 7.

18 Virilio, *Bunker Archeology*, p. 44.

19 Ibid.

20 Tom Vanderbilt, *Survival City: Adventures Among the Ruins of Atomic America* (Princeton, NJ, 2002), p. 16.

21 Ibid., p. 124.

22 See, for example, Richard Sauder, *Underground Bases and Tunnels: What is the Government Trying to Hide?* (Kempton, IL, 1996).

23 Virilio, *Bunker Archeology*, p. 44.

24 Paul Hirst, *Space and Power: Politics, War and Architecture* (Cambridge, 2005), p. 215.

25 Andreas Huyssen, 'Nostalgia for Ruins', *Grey Room*, XXIII (2006), pp. 6–21, p. 8.

26 Brian Dillon, 'Decline and Fall', *Frieze*, CXXX (April 2010), https://frieze.com.

27 Svetlana Boym, *The Future of Nostalgia* (New York, 2001), p. 41.

28 Ibid., pp. 41, 49.

29 Huyssen, 'Nostalgia for Ruins', p. 8.

30 Ibid., p. 10.

31 Cathy Caruth, *Unclaimed Experience: Trauma, Narrative, and History* (Baltimore, MD, 1996), p. 7.

32 See, for example, Bernard Lowry, *20th Century Defences in Britain: An Introductory Guide*, Practical Handbooks in Archaeology No. 12, revd edn (York, 1998); William Foot, *The Battlefields That Nearly Were: Defended England 1940* (Stroud, 2006); William Foot,

Beaches, Fields, Streets, and Hills: The Anti-invasion Landscapes of England, 1940 (York, 2006); Mike Osborne, *Defending Britain: Twentieth-century Military Structures in the Landscape* (Stroud, 2004); Mike Osborne, *Pillboxes of Britain and Ireland* (Stroud, 2008). The Royal Commission on the Historical Monuments of England conducted a similar project in 1999 that dealt with Cold War buildings. See Wayne D. Cocroft and Roger J. C. Thomas, *Cold War: Building for Nuclear Confrontation, 1946–89* (Swindon, 2003).

33 Rudi Rolf, *Atlantikwall-Typenheft / Atlantic Wall Typology / Typologie du Mur de l'Atlantique* (Middleburg, VA, 2008).

34 John Schofield, *Combat Archaeology: Material Culture and Modern Conflict* (London, 2005), p. 171.

35 Don DeLillo, *Underworld* (London, 1997), p. 248.

36 Wayne Cocroft and John Schofield, eds, *A Fearsome Heritage: Diverse Legacies of the Cold War* (Walnut Creek, CA, 2007). For a discussion of Orford Ness as the venue for site-specific art, see Caitlin DeSilvey, 'Palliative Curation: Art and Entropy on Orford Ness', in *Ruin Memories: Materialities, Aesthetics and the Archaeology of the Recent Past*, ed. Bjørnar Olsen and Þóra Pétursdóttir (Abingdon, 2014), pp. 79–91.

37 Louise K. Wilson, 'Notes on A Record of Fear: On the Threshold of the Audible', *Leonardo Music Journal*, XVI (2006), pp. 28–33.

38 Simon Guy, 'Shadow Architectures: War, Memories, and Berlin's Future', in *Cities, War, and Terrorism: Towards an Urban Geopolitics*, ed. Stephen Graham (Oxford, 2004), pp. 75–92, p. 75.

39 On bunker busters, see Benjamin Phelan, 'Buried Truth: Debunking the Nuclear "Bunker Buster"', *Harper's Magazine* (December 2004), pp. 70–72.

40 On the contemporary cultural significance of Cold War bunkers, see the essays collected in Luke Bennett, ed., *In the Ruins of the Cold War Bunker: Affect, Materiality and Meaning Making* (London, 2017).

41 John McPhee, *La Place de la Concorde Suisse* (New York, 1984), p. 3.

42 Ibid., p. 54.

43 See Yitzhak Greenberg, 'The Swiss Armed Forces as a Model for the IDF Reserve System – Indeed?', *Israel Studies*, XVIII/3 (2013), pp. 95–111.

44 McPhee, *La Place*, p. 3.

45 Ibid., p. 4.

46 Ibid., p. 56.

47 Ibid., p. 57.

48 Ibid., p. 63.

49 Ibid., p. 11.

50 J. F. Hardy, 'Ascent of the Finsteraar Horn', in *Peaks, Passes, and Glaciers, being Excursions by Members of the Alpine Club*, 5th edn, ed. John Ball (London, 1860), pp. 198–215, p. 204.
51 McPhee, *La Place*, p. 11.
52 Ibid., p. 21.
53 Ibid., p. 14.
54 Ibid., pp. 21, 22.
55 Ibid., p. 130.
56 Ibid., p. 25.
57 Ibid., p. 23.
58 Ibid., p. 93.
59 Ibid., pp. 23, 22.

5 The General Was Rubbish in the End

1 Andreas Huyssen, *Twilight Memories: Marking Time in a Culture of Amnesia* (New York, 1995), p. 250.
2 Robert Musil, 'Monuments', in *Posthumous Papers of a Living Author*, trans. Peter Wortsman (Brooklyn, NY, 2006), pp. 64–8, p. 64.
3 Ibid., p. 65.
4 Ibid., p. 67.
5 Ibid., p. 68.
6 Ibid.
7 Mark Lewis, 'What is to be Done?', in *Ideology and Power in the Age of Lenin in Ruins*, ed. Arthur Kroker and Marilouise Kroker (New York, 1991), pp. 1–18, p. 2.
8 Ibid., p. 3.
9 Ibid.
10 Thomas Carlyle, 'Hudson's Statue', in *Latter Day Pamphlets* (London, 1850), pp. 216–48, p. 217.
11 John Berger, *Art and Revolution: Ernst Neizvestny, Endurance, and the Role of Art* (New York, 1997), p. 75.
12 Michael North, *The Final Sculpture: Public Monuments and Modern Poems* (Ithaca, NY, 1985), pp. 29–30.
13 Kirk Savage, *Monument Wars: Washington, DC, the National Mall, and the Transformation of the Memorial Landscape* (Berkeley, CA, 2009), p. 10.
14 Kenneth Gross, *The Dream of the Moving Statue* (Ithaca, NY, 1992), p. 16.
15 Ibid.
16 Ibid., p. 22. See also Michel Serres, *Statues: The Second Book of Foundations*, trans. Randolph Burks (London, 2015).
17 Henry James, *The American Scene* (London, 1907), pp. 173–4.

18 'Reagan Statue Unveiled in Capitol Rotunda', *San Gabriel Valley Tribune*, www.sgvtribune.com, 9 June 2009.
19 Garry Wills, *Reagan's America: Innocents at Home* (New York, 2000), p. xxiv.
20 Wallace Stevens, 'The Noble Rider and the Sound of Words', in *The Necessary Angel: Essays on Reality and the Imagination* (New York, 1951), pp. 1–36, pp. 4, 6.
21 Ibid., p. 7.
22 Ibid., p. 11.
23 Alexis de Tocqueville, quoted in Rob Wilson, *American Sublime: The Genealogy of a Poetic Genre* (Madison, WI, 1991), p. 175.
24 Wallace Stevens, *The Collected Poems* (New York, 1971), p. 472.
25 Ibid., pp. 390–91. See also Harold Bloom's gloss, 'every image is on the dump, and the only change the statue ever will know is the final transformation into rubbish.' Harold Bloom, *Wallace Stevens: The Poems of Our Climate* (Ithaca, NY, 1980), pp. 192–3.
26 Frank O'Hara, *The Selected Poems of Frank O'Hara*, ed. Donald Allen (New York, 1974), p. 175.
27 Stevens, *Collected Poems*, p. 482.
28 Leslie George Katz, 'The American Monument', in Lee Friedlander, *The American Monument* (New York, 2017), unpaginated.
29 Ibid.
30 Howard Zinn, *A People's History of the United States, 1492–Present*, 3rd edn (New York, 2013), p. 684.
31 North, *The Final Sculpture*, p. 27.
32 Laura Mulvey, 'Reflections on Disgraced Monuments', in *Architecture and Revolution: Contemporary Perspectives on Central and Eastern Europe*, ed. Neil Leach (London, 1999), pp. 219–27, p. 221.
33 Ibid., p. 222.
34 Mark Lewis, quoted ibid., p. 223.
35 Ibid.
36 Ibid.

Conclusion

1 Neil MacGregor, quoted in Susan Neiman, *Learning from the Germans: Confronting Race and the Memory of Evil* (London, 2019), p. 31.

BIBLIOGRAPHY

Abrams, Lynn, 'Revisiting Akenfield: Forty Years of an Iconic Text',
    Oral History, XXXVII/1 (2009), pp. 33–42
—, *Oral History Theory* (Abingdon, 2010)
Anderson, Kay, Mona Domosh, Steve Pile and Nigel Thrift, eds,
    Handbook of Cultural Geography (London, 2003)
Apel, Dora, *Beautiful Terrible Ruins: Detroit and the Anxiety of Decline*
    (New Brunswick, NJ, 2015)
Aragon, Louis, *Paris Peasant*, trans. Simon Watson Taylor (Boston,
    MA, 1994)
Austin, Dan, *Lost Detroit: Stories Behind the Motor City's Majestic Ruins*
    (Charleston, SC, 2010)
Banham, Reyner, *A Concrete Atlantis: U.S. Industrial Building and
    European Modern Architecture, 1900–1925* (Cambridge, MA, 1989)
Bauman, Zygmunt, *Modernity and Ambivalence* (Cambridge, 1991)
Benjamin, Walter, *The Arcades Project*, trans. Howard Eiland
    (Cambridge, MA, 2002)
Bennett, James, 'A Tribute To Ruin Irks Detroit', www.nytimes.com,
    10 December 1995
Bennett, Luke, ed., *In the Ruins of the Cold War Bunker: Affect,
    Materiality and Meaning Making* (London, 2017)
Berger, Alan, *Drosscape: Wasting Land in Urban America* (Princeton,
    NJ, 2006)
Berger, Jenna, 'Nuclear Tourism and the Manhattan Project', *Columbia
    Journal of American Studies,* XII (2006), pp. 196–214
Berger, John, *Art and Revolution: Ernst Neizvestny, Endurance, and the
    Role of Art* (New York, 1997)
Bloch, Ernst, 'Nonsynchronism and the Obligation to Its Dialectics',
    trans. Mark Ritter, *New German Critique*, XI (1977), pp. 22–38
—, *Heritage of Our Times*, trans. Neville and Stephen Plaice
    (Cambridge, 1991)

Bloom, Harold, *Wallace Stevens: The Poems of Our Climate*
      (Ithaca, NY, 1980)
Blythe, Ronald, *Akenfield: Portrait of an English Village* (London, 2005)
—, and Peter Hall, 'Home Movie: The Filming of *Akenfield*', *The
      Countryman*, LXXVIII/2 (1973), pp. 113–21
Bonnett, Alastair, 'The Dilemmas of Radical Nostalgia in British Psycho-
      geography', *Theory, Culture and Society*, XXVI/1 (2009), pp. 45–70
—, *Left in the Past: Radicalism and the Politics of Nostalgia*
      (London, 2010)
Boyes, Georgina, *The Imagined Village: Culture, Ideology and the
      English Folk Revival*, revd edn (Leeds, 2010)
Boym, Svetlana, *The Future of Nostalgia* (New York, 2001)
Brocken, Michael, *The British Folk Revival, 1944–2002*
      (Aldershot, 2003)
Brownlow, Kevin, *Winstanley: Warts and All* (London, 2009)
Brubach, Holly, 'Ruin With a View', *New York Times Magazine*,
      www.nytimes.com, 9 April 2010
Buck, Louisa, 'Powerful, Political and Pungent: Mike Nelson's Tate
      Britain Commission', *Art Newspaper*, www.theartnewspaper.com,
      20 March 2019
Bunge, William, *Fitzgerald: The Geography of a Revolution*
      (Cambridge, MA, 1971)
Bureau of Labor Statistics, 'Local Area Unemployment Statistics:
      Unemployment Rates for the 50 Largest Cities (Based on Census
      2000 Population)', www.bls.gov, accessed 1 November 2019
Byles, Jeff, *Rubble: Unearthing the History of Demolition*
      (New York, 2005)
Carlyle, Thomas, 'Hudson's Statue', in *Latter Day Pamphlets* (London,
      1850), pp. 216–48
Carty, Sharon Silke, 'Michigan Tax Credit Courts Film Industry to
      Lure Money, Jobs', *USA Today*, www.usatoday.com, 17 August 2009
Caruth, Cathy, *Unclaimed Experience: Trauma, Narrative, and History*
      (Baltimore, MD, 1996)
Chiarella, Tom, 'The Most Important Movie of the Year', *Esquire*
      (June 2009), pp. 87–91
Chozick, Amy, 'Motown Becomes Movietown', *Wall Street Journal*,
      http://online.wsj.com, 17 September 2010
Cocker, Mark, 'Death of the Naturalist: Why Is the "New Nature
      Writing" So Tame?', *New Statesman*, www.newstatesman.com,
      17 June 2015
Cocroft, Wayne, and John Schofield, eds, *A Fearsome Heritage: Diverse
      Legacies of the Cold War* (Walnut Creek, CA, 2007)
Cocroft, Wayne D., and Roger J. C. Thomas, *Cold War: Building for
      Nuclear Confrontation, 1946–89* (Swindon, 2003)

Corkin, Stanley, *Starring New York: Filming the Grime and the Glamour of the Long 1970s* (New York, 2011)

Correia, Alice, 'Interpreting Jeremy Deller's The Battle of Orgreave', *Visual Culture in Britain*, XII/2 (2006), pp. 93–112

Cowley, Jason, 'Editors' Letter: The New Nature Writing', *Granta*, CII (2008), pp. 7–12

Cull, Nicholas J., 'Peter Watkins' *Culloden* and the Alternative Form in Historical Filmmaking', in *Retrovisions: Reinventing the Past in Film and Fiction*, ed. Deborah Cartmell, I. Q. Hunter and Imelda Whelehan (London, 2001), pp. 87–101

Cumming, Laura, 'Mike Nelson: The Asset Strippers Review – His All-time Masterpiece', *The Observer*, www.theguardian.com, 24 March 2019

Davis, Colin, 'État Présent: Hauntology, Spectres and Phantoms', *French Studies*, LIX/3 (2005), pp. 373–9

Davis, Sophia, *Island Thinking: Suffolk's Stories of Landscape, Militarisation and Identity* (London, 2019)

DeLillo, Don, *Underworld* (London, 1997)

Deller, Jeremy, *The English Civil War, Part II: Personal Accounts of the 1984–85 Miners' Strike* (London, 2001)

Derrida, Jacques, *Spectres of Marx: The State of the Debt, the Work of Mourning, and the New International*, trans. Peggy Kamuf (New York, 1994)

DeSilvey, Caitlin, 'Palliative Curation: Art and Entropy on Orford Ness', in *Ruin Memories: Materialities, Aesthetics and the Archaeology of the Recent Past*, ed. Bjørnar Olsen and Þóra Pétursdóttir (Abingdon, 2014), pp. 79–91

Diller, Elizabeth, and Ricardo Scofidio, eds, *Back to the Front: Tourisms of War* (Princeton, NJ, 1996)

Dillon, Brian, 'Decline and Fall', *Frieze*, CXXX (April 2010), www.frieze.com

—, ed., *Ruins*, Documents of Contemporary Art (London, 2011)

Edensor, Tim, *Industrial Ruins: Spaces, Aesthetics and Materiality* (Oxford, 2005)

Elzanowski, Jerzy, 'Manufacturing Ruins: Architecture and Representation in Post-catastrophic Warsaw', *Journal of Architecture*, XV/1 (2010), pp. 67–82

Farley, Paul, and Michael Symmons Roberts, *Edgelands: Journeys into England's True Wilderness* (London, 2011)

Farquharson, Alex, 'Jeremy Deller: The Battle of Orgreave, London, UK', *Frieze*, LXI (September 2001), www.frieze.com

Fisher, Mark, 'What is Hauntology?,' *Film Quarterly*, LXVI/1 (2012), pp. 16–24

—, *Ghosts of My Life: Writings on Depression, Hauntology and Lost Futures* (Winchester, 2014)

Flam, Jack, ed., *Robert Smithson: The Collected Writings* (Berkeley, CA, 1996)

Foot, William, *The Battlefields That Nearly Were: Defended England 1940* (Stroud, 2006)

—, *Beaches, Fields, Streets, and Hills: The Anti-invasion Landscapes of England, 1940* (York, 2006)

Ford, Laura Oldfield, *Savage Messiah* (London, 2011)

Freud, Sigmund, *Totem and Taboo: Resemblances between the Psychic Lives of Savages and Neurotics*, trans. A. A. Brill (New York, 1919)

Friedlander, Lee, *The American Monument* (New York, 2017)

Fritzsche, Peter, 'Specters of History: On Nostalgia, Exile, and Modernity', *American Historical Review*, CVI/5 (2001), pp. 1587–618

Frow, John, 'Tourism and the Semiotics of Nostalgia', *October*, LVII (1991), pp. 123–51

Gallagher, John, *Revolution Detroit: Strategies for Urban Reinvention* (Detroit, MI, 2013)

Gane, Mike, 'Paul Virilio's Bunker Theorizing', in *Paul Virilio: From Modernism to Hypermodernism and Beyond*, ed. John Armitage (London, 2000), pp. 85–102

Garrett, Bradley, *Explore Everything: Place-hacking the City* (London, 2013)

Gentry, Kynan, '"The Pathos of Conservation": Raphael Samuel and the Politics of Heritage', *International Journal of Heritage Studies*, XXI/6 (2015), pp. 561–76

Gerard, Greg, *Phantom Shanghai* (Toronto, 2010)

Gilbert, David, 'The English Civil War Part II: Personal Accounts of the 1984–85 Miners' Strike by Jeremy Deller', *Oral History*, XXXIII/1 (2005), pp. 104–5

Ginsberg, Allen, *Collected Poems, 1947–1997* (New York, 2007)

Gordillo, Gastón, *Rubble: The Afterlife of Destruction* (Durham, NC, 2014)

Graham, Stephen, ed., *Cities, War, and Terrorism: Towards an Urban Geopolitics* (Oxford, 2004)

Greenberg, Yitzhak, 'The Swiss Armed Forces as a Model for the IDF Reserve System – Indeed?', *Israel Studies*, XVIII/3 (2013), pp. 95–111

Greenburg, Z. O'Malley, 'America's Most Dangerous Cities', *Forbes*, www.forbes.com, 23 April 2009

Gross, Kenneth, *The Dream of the Moving Statue* (Ithaca, NY, 1992)

Gumbrecht, Hans Ulrich, *After 1945: Latency as Origin of the Present* (Stanford, CA, 2013)

Guy, Simon, 'Shadow Architectures: War, Memories, and Berlin's Future', in *Cities, War, and Terrorism: Towards an Urban Geopolitics*, ed. Stephen Graham (Oxford, 2004), pp. 75–92

Hardy, J. F, 'Ascent of the Finsteraar Horn', in *Peaks, Passes, and Glaciers, being Excursions by Members of the Alpine Club*, 5th edn, ed. John Ball (London, 1860), pp. 198–215

Hatherley, Owen, *Militant Modernism* (London, 2009)

—, *A Guide to the New Ruins of Great Britain* (London, 2010)

—, 'After the Heygate Estate, A Grey Future Awaits', *The Guardian*, www.guardian.co.uk, 8 February 2011

—, *The Ministry of Nostalgia: Consuming Austerity* (London, 2016)

Heartfield, John, 'Londonostalgia', www.heartfield.org, accessed 1 November 2019

Hebdige, Dick, *Subculture: The Meaning of Style* (London, 1979)

Hell, Julia, 'Ruins Travel: Orphic Journeys through Germany's Ruins', in *Writing Travel*, ed. John Zilcosky (Baltimore, MD, 2008), pp. 123–60

Hell, Julia, and Andreas Schönle, eds, *Ruins of Modernity* (Durham, NC, 2010)

Herscher, Andrew, *The Unreal Estate Guide to Detroit* (Ann Arbor, MI, 2012)

Hewison, Robert, *The Heritage Industry: Britain in a Climate of Decline* (London, 1987)

—, *Cultural Capital: The Rise and Fall of Creative Britain* (London, 2014)

Hirst, Paul, *Space and Power: Politics, War and Architecture* (Cambridge, 2005)

Hobsbawm, Eric, and Terence Ranger, *The Invention of Tradition* [1982] (Cambridge, 1992)

Horvath, Ronald J., 'The Detroit Geographical Expedition and Institute Experience', *Antipode*, III/1 (November 1971), pp. 73–85

Howkins, Alun, 'Inventing Everyman: George Ewart Evans, Oral History and National Identity', *Oral History*, XXV (1994), pp. 26–32

Huyssen, Andreas, *Twilight Memories: Marking Time in a Culture of Amnesia* (New York, 1995)

—, 'Present Pasts: Media, Politics, Amnesia', *Public Culture*, XII/1 (2000), pp. 21–38

—, 'Nostalgia for Ruins', *Grey Room*, XXIII (2006), pp. 6–21

James, David, *Contemporary British Fiction and the Artistry of Space: Style, Landscape, Perception* (London, 2009)

James, Henry, *The American Scene* [1903] (London, 1907)

Jamie, Kathleen, 'A Lone Enraptured Male: Review: The Wild Places by Robert Macfarlane', *London Review of Books*, XXX/5 (6 March 2008), pp. 25–7

Judah, Hettie, 'Fire Sale Britain: Mike Nelson on Why he Turned the Tate into a Big Salvage Yard', *The Guardian*, www.theguardian.com, 18 March 2019

Katz, Bruce, and Jeremy Nowak, *The New Localism: How Cities Can Thrive in the Age of Populism* (Washington, DC, 2018)

Kennedy, Liam, *Race and Urban Space in American Culture* (Edinburgh, 2000)

Kennedy, Peter, Harry Cox and Francis Collinson, 'Harry Cox: English Folk Singer', *Journal of the English Folk Dance and Song Society*, VIII/3 (December 1958), pp. 142–55

Kinder, Kimberley, DIY *Detroit: Making Do in a City Without Services* (Minneapolis, MN, 2016)

Kinney, Rebecca J., *Beautiful Wasteland: The Rise of Detroit as America's Postindustrial Frontier* (Minneapolis, MN, 2016)

Kitamura, Katie, 'Recreating Chaos: Jeremy Deller's *The Battle of Orgreave*', in *Historical Reenactment: From Realism to the Affective Turn*, ed. Iain McCalman and Paul A. Pickering (Basingstoke, 2010), pp. 39–49

Lennon, John, and Malcolm Foley, *Dark Tourism: The Attraction of Death and Disaster* (London, 2000)

Lewis, Mark, 'What Is to Be Done?', in *Ideology and Power in the Age of Lenin in Ruins*, ed. Arthur Kroker and Marilouise Kroker (New York, 1991), pp. 1–18

Lewis, Tom, 'The Politics of "Hauntology" in Derrida's *Specters of Marx*', *Rethinking Marxism*, IX/3 (1996), pp. 19–39

Lichtenstein, Rachel, *Estuary: Out from London to the Sea* (London, 2016)

Linehan, Denis, 'An Archaeology of Dereliction: Poetics and Policy in the Governing of Depressed Industrial Districts in Interwar England and Wales', *Journal of Historical Geography*, XXVI/1 (2000), pp. 99–113

Lowenthal, David, *The Heritage Crusade and the Spoils of History* (Cambridge, 1998)

—, *The Past is a Foreign Country – Revisited* (Cambridge, 2015)

Lowry, Bernard, *20th Century Defences in Britain: An Introductory Guide*, Practical Handbooks in Archaeology No. 12, revd edn (York, 1998)

Luckhurst, Roger, 'The Contemporary London Gothic and the Limits of the "Spectral Turn"', *Textual Practice*, XVI/3 (2002), pp. 527–46

Mabey, Richard, *The Unofficial Countryside* [1973] (Wimborne Minster, 2010)

—, *Weeds: How Vagabond Plants Gatecrashed Civilisation and Changed the Way We Think about Nature* (London, 2010)

Macaulay, Rose, *Pleasure of Ruins* (London, 1953)

MacDonald, Christine, 'Suburbs Gain While Detroit Population Drops Below 700,000', *Detroit News*, www.detroitnews, 21 May 2014

Macfarlane, Robert, 'A Road of One's Own: Past and Present Artists of the Randomly Motivated Walk', *Times Literary Supplement* (7 October 2005), pp. 3–4

—, *The Wild Places* (London, 2007)

—, 'Ghost Species', *Granta*, CII, The New Nature Writing (2008), pp. 109–28

—, *Landmarks* (London, 2015)

—, 'Why We Need Nature Writing', *New Statesman*, www.newstatesman.com, 2 September 2015

Macfarlane, Robert, and Jackie Morris, *The Lost Words* (London, 2017)

McGraw, Bill, 'Life in the Ruins of Detroit', *History Workshop Journal*, LXIII (2007), pp. 288–302

McPhee, John, *La Place de la Concorde Suisse* (New York, 1984)

Mallory, Keith, and Arvid Ottar, *Architecture of Aggression: A History of Military Architecture in North West Europe, 1900–1945* (London, 1973)

Marchand, Yves, and Romain Meffre, *The Ruins of Detroit* (Göttingen, 2010)

Margaine, Sylvain, *Forbidden Places: Exploring our Abandoned Heritage* (Versailles, 2009)

Marsh, Jan, 'Review: A Miraculous Relic?', *Cambridge Quarterly*, VI/1 (1972), pp. 70–77

Matless, David, *Landscape and Englishness* (London, 1998)

Metropolitan Observatory for Digital Cultural and Representation, www.modcar.org, accessed 1 November 2019

Michigan Film Production, www.michiganfilmproduction.com, accessed 1 November 2019

Minton, Anna, 'The Price of Regeneration', *Places*, https://placesjournal.org, September 2018

Mitchell, Don, 'Dead Labor and the Political Economy of Landscape – California Living, California Dying', in *The Handbook of Cultural Geography*, ed. Kay Anderson, Mona Domosh, Steve Pile and Nigel Thrift (London, 2003), pp. 233–48

Mitchell, W.J.T, 'Introduction', in *Landscape and Power*, ed. W.J.T. Mitchell (Chicago, IL, 1994), pp. 1–4

Moore, Andrew, *Detroit Disassembled* (Bologna and Akron, OH, 2010)

Moran, Joe, *Reading the Everyday* (Abingdon, 2005)

—, 'A Cultural History of the New Nature Writing', *Literature and History*, XXIII/1 (2014), pp. 49–63

Mulvey, Laura, 'Reflections on Disgraced Monuments', in *Architecture and Revolution: Contemporary Perspectives on Central and Eastern Europe*, ed. Neil Leach (London, 1999), pp. 219–27

Munroe, J., and S. Gerard, *Sword of My Mouth: A Post-rapture Graphic Novel* (San Diego, CA, 2010)

Musil, Robert, 'Monuments', in *Posthumous Papers of a Living Author*, trans. Peter Wortsman (Brooklyn, NY, 2006), pp. 64–8

Neiman, Susan, *Learning from the Germans: Confronting Race and the Memory of Evil* (London, 2019)

Newby, Howard, 'Akenfield Revisited', *Oral History*, III/1 (1975), pp. 76–83

Newland, Paul, *British Films of the 1970s* (Manchester, 2015)

Ninjalicious, *Access All Areas: A User's Guide to the Art of Urban Exploration* (Toronto, 2005)

North, Michael, *The Final Sculpture: Public Monuments and Modern Poems* (Ithaca, NY, 1985)

O'Hagan, Sean, 'Detroit in Ruins', *The Observer*, www.theguardian.com, 2 January 2011

O'Hara, Frank, *The Selected Poems of Frank O'Hara*, ed. Donald Allen (New York, 1974)

Osborne, Mike, *Defending Britain: Twentieth-century Military Structures in the Landscape* (Stroud, 2004)

—, *Pillboxes of Britain and Ireland* (Stroud, 2008)

Phelan, Benjamin, 'Buried Truth: Debunking the Nuclear "Bunker Buster"', *Harper's Magazine* (December 2004), pp. 70–72

Philby, Charlotte, 'Living in Ghostland: The Last Heygate Residents', *The Independent*, www.independent.co.uk, 29 March 2010

Philp, Drew, *A $500 House in Detroit: Rebuilding an Abandoned Home and an American City* (New York, 2017)

Pinder, David, 'Arts of Urban Exploration', *Cultural Geographies*, XII (2005), pp. 383–411

Powell, Hillary, and Isaac Marrero-Guillamón, *The Art of Dissent: Adventures in London's Olympic State* (London, 2012)

Quin, John, 'Everything Must Go: Mike Nelson Inters British Industry', *The Quietus*, https://thequietus.com, 30 March 2019

Rabinbach, Anson, 'Unclaimed Heritage: Ernst Bloch's Heritage of Our Times and the Theory of Fascism', *New German Critique*, XI (1977), pp. 5–21

Reynolds, Ann, *Robert Smithson: Learning from New Jersey and Elsewhere* (Cambridge, MA, 2004)

Reynolds, Simon, *Retromania: Pop Culture's Addiction to its Own Past* (London, 2011)

Rolf, Rudi, *Atlantikwall-Typenheft / Atlantic Wall Typology / Typologie du Mur de l'Atlantique* (Middleburg, VA, 2008)

Rubenstein, Lenny, '*Winstanley* and the Historical Film: An Interview with Kevin Brownlow', *Cinéaste*, X/4 (Fall 1980), pp. 22–5

Ryle, Martin, 'After "Organic Community": Ecocriticism, Nature, and Human Nature', in *The Environmental Tradition in English Literature*, ed. John Parham (Aldershot, 2002), pp. 11–14

Salerno, Roger A., *Landscapes of Abandonment: Capitalism, Modernity, and Estrangement* (Albany, NY, 2005)

Samuel, Raphael, *Theatres of Memory: Past and Present in Contemporary Culture*, vol. I (London, 1994)

—, 'Perils of the Transcript' (1971), in *The Oral History Reader*, ed. Robert Perks and Alistair Thomson (London, 1998), pp. 389–92

Samuel, Raphael, Barbara Bloomfield and Guy Boanas, eds, *The Enemy Within: Pit Villages and the Miners' Strike of 1984–5* (London, 1986)

Sauder, Richard, *Underground Bases and Tunnels: What Is the Government Trying to Hide?* (Kempton, IL, 1996)

Savage, Jon, *England's Dreaming: The Sex Pistols and Punk Rock* (London, 2005)

—, 'The Things That Aren't There Anymore', *Critical Quarterly*, L/1–2 (2008), pp. 180–97

Savage, Kirk, *Monument Wars: Washington DC, the National Mall, and the Transformation of the Memorial Landscape* (Berkeley, CA, 2009)

—, 'The Obsolescence of Sculpture', *American Art*, XXIV/1 (2010), pp. 9–14

Schofield, John, *Combat Archaeology: Material Culture and Modern Conflict* (London, 2005)

—, *Aftermath: Readings in the Archaeology of Recent Conflict* (New York, 2009)

Schofield, John, William Gray Johnson and Colleen M. Beck, eds, *Matériel Culture: The Archaeology of 20th Century Conflict* (New York, 2002)

Schwartz, Frederic J., 'Ernst Bloch and Wilhelm Pinder: Out of Sync', *Grey Room*, III (2001), pp. 54–89

Sebald, W. G., *The Rings of Saturn*, trans. Michael Hulse (London, 1998)

—, *Austerlitz*, trans. Anthea Bell (London, 2002)

Serres, Michel, *Statues: The Second Book of Foundations*, trans. Randolph Burks (London, 2015)

Shoard, Marion, 'Edgelands', in *Remaking the Landscape: The Changing Face of Britain*, ed. Jennifer Jenkins (London, 2002), pp. 117–46

—, 'Review: *Edgelands: Journeys into England's True Wilderness* by Paul Farley and Michael Symmons Roberts', *The Guardian*, www.theguardian.com, 6 March 2011

Sinclair, Iain, *Downriver (or, The Vessels of Wrath): A Narrative in Twelve Tales* (London, 1991)

—, *Lights out for the Territory: 9 Excursions in the Secret History of London* (London, 1997)

—, *Sorry Meniscus: Excursions to the Millennium Dome* (London, 1999)
—, *London Orbital: A Walk Around the M25* (London, 2002)
—, *Edge of the Orison: In the Traces of John Clare's 'Journey out of Essex'*
    (London, 2005)
—, ed., *London: City of Disappearances* (London, 2007)
—, 'The Olympics Scam', *London Review of Books*, XXX/12
    (19 June 2008), pp. 17–23
—, *Hackney, That Rose-red Empire: A Confidential Report*
    (London, 2010)
—, *Ghost Milk: Calling Time on the Grand Project* (London, 2011)
Smith, Jos, *The New Nature Writing: Rethinking the Literature of Place*
    (London, 2017)
Smithson, Robert, 'A Tour of the Monuments of Passaic, New Jersey
    (1967)', in *Robert Smithson: The Collected Writings*, ed. Jack Flam
    (Berkeley, CA, 1995), pp. 68–74
Snell, K.D.M., *Spirits of Community: English Senses of Belonging and
    Loss, 1750–2000* (London, 2016)
Solà-Morales, Ignasi de, 'Terrain Vague', in *Anyplace*, ed. Cynthia C.
    Davidson (Cambridge, MA, 1995), pp. 118–23
Solnit, Rebecca, 'Detroit Arcadia: Exploring the Post-American
    Landscape', *Harper's Magazine* (July 2007), pp. 65–73
Soper, Kate, 'The Limits of Hauntology', in 'Spectres of Derrida:
    Symposium', *Radical Philosophy*, LXXV (January/February 1996),
    pp. 26–31
Sprinker, Michael, ed., *Ghostly Demarcations: A Symposium on Jacques
    Derrida's Specters of Marx* (London, 1999)
Steinhauser, Jillian, 'Finishing "Mobile Homestead" After the Death
    of the Artist', *Hyperallergic*, http://hyperallergic.com, 17 May 2012
Steinmetz, George, 'Harrowed Landscapes: White Ruingazers in
    Namibia and Detroit and the Cultivation of Memory', *Visual
    Studies*, XXIII (2008), pp. 211–37
—, 'Guest Editorial', *Environment and Planning D: Society and Space*,
    XXVII (2009), pp. 761–70
Steinmetz, George, and Michael Chanan, 'Drive-by Shooting: Filming
    Detroit: Interviews with the Filmmakers' (2005),
    www.detroitruinofacity.com, accessed 1 November 2019
Stevens, Wallace, 'The Noble Rider and the Sound of Words', in
    The Necessary Angel: Essays on Reality and the Imagination
    (New York, 1951), pp. 1–36
—, *The Collected Poems* (New York, 1971)
Sugrue, Thomas J., *The Origins of the Urban Crisis: Race and Inequality
    in Postwar Detroit* (Princeton, NJ, 1996)
Sullivan, Amy, 'Postcard from Detroit', *Time*, https://time.com,
    April 2009

Temple, Julien, 'Directors Statement', *Oil City Confidential Production Notes* (2009), www.filmfestival.be, accessed 12 October 2010

Thompson, E. P., 'History from Below', *Times Literary Supplement* (7 April 1966), pp. 279–80

Thompson, Paul, *The Voice of the Past: Oral History*, 3rd edn (Oxford, 2000)

Tibbetts, John C., 'Kevin Brownlow's Historical Films: *It Happened Here* (1965) and *Winstanley* (1975)', *Historical Journal of Film, Radio and Television*, xx/2 (2000), pp. 227–51

——, '*Winstanley*; or, Kevin Brownlow Camps Out on St George's Hill', *Literature/Film Quarterly*, xxxi/4 (2003), pp. 312–18

Vanderbilt, Tom, *Survival City: Adventures Among the Ruins of Atomic America* (Princeton, NJ, 2002)

Vergara, Camilo José, 'Downtown Detroit: American Acropolis or Vacant Land?', *Metropolis* (April 1995), pp. 33–8

——, *The New American Ghetto* (New Brunswick, NJ, 1995)

——, *American Ruins* (New York, 1999)

Vine, Richard, 'Taiwan's New Bunker Museum', *Art in America*, vi (2005), p. 49

Virilio, Paul, *Bunker Archeology*, trans. George Collins (Princeton, NJ, 1994)

Walker, Peter, 'South London's Heygate Estate Mourned by Locals – and Hollywood', *The Guardian*, www.theguardian.com, 3 September 2010

Watten, Barrett, 'Learning from Detroit: The Poetics of Ruined Space', *Detroit Research* (2014), www.detroitresearch.org, accessed 1 November 2019

Weisman, Alan, *The World Without Us* (London, 2008)

Williams, Raymond, *The Country and the City* (Oxford, 1973)

Wills, Garry, *Reagan's America: Innocents at Home* (New York, 2000)

Wilson, Louise K., 'Notes on A Record of Fear: On the Threshold of the Audible', *Leonardo Music Journal*, xvi (2006), pp. 28–33

Wilson, Rob, *American Sublime: The Genealogy of a Poetic Genre* (Madison, WI, 1991)

Wohlfarth, Irving, 'Et Cetera? The Historian as Chiffonnier', *New German Critique*, xxxix (Autumn 1986), pp. 142–68

Woodward, Christopher, *In Ruins* (London, 2002)

Worpole, Ken, and Jason Orton, *350 Miles: An Essex Journey* (Colchester, 2005)

——, *The New English Landscape* (London, 2013)

Wright, Patrick, *On Living in an Old Country: The National Past in Contemporary Britain* (London, 1985)

——, *A Journey Through Ruins: The Last Days of London* (London, 1991)

Wright, Patrick, and Jeremy Davis, 'Just Start Digging: Memory and the Framing of Heritage', *Memory Studies*, III/3 (2010), pp. 196–203

Yablon, Nick, *Untimely Ruins: An Archaeology of American Urban Modernity, 1819–1919* (Chicago, IL, 2009)

Young, James E., 'The Counter-monument: Memory Against itself in Germany Today', *Critical Inquiry*, XVIII/2 (1996), pp. 267–96

Young, Rob, *Electric Eden: Unearthing Britain's Visionary Music* (London, 2010)

Zalasiewicz, Jan, *The Earth After Us: What Legacy Will Humans Leave in the Rocks?* (Oxford, 2008)

Zinn, Howard, *A People's History of the United States, 1492–Present*, 3rd edn (New York, 2013)

Zucker, Paul, *Fascination of Decay: Ruins: Relic – Symbol – Ornament* (Ridgewood, NJ, 1968)

Zweite, Armin, ed., *Bernd and Hiller Becher, Typologies* (Cambridge, MA, 2004)

Filmography

8 Mile. Dir. Curtis Hanson. 2002.

Akenfield. Dir. Peter Hall. 1974.

Burn. Dir. Tom Putnam and Brenna Sanchez. 2012.

Control. Dir. Anton Corbijn. 2007.

Culloden. Dir. Peter Watkins. 1964.

Death Wish. Dir. Michael Winner. 1974.

Detroit Lives. Dir. Thalia Mavros. 2010.

Detroit: Ruin of a City. Dir. Michael Chanan and George Steinmetz. 2005.

Detroit Wild City. Dir. Florent Tillon. 2010.

Detropia. Dir. Heidi Ewing and Rachel Grady. 2012.

Dirty Harry. Dir. Don Siegel. 1971.

Disgraced Monuments. Dir. Mark Lewis and Laura Mulvey. 1994.

Get Carter. Dir. Mike Hodges. 1971.

Gran Torino. Dir. Clint Eastwood. 2008.

Harry Brown. Dir. Daniel Barber. 2009.

Hereafter. Dir. Clint Eastwood. 2010.

Ill Manors. Dir. Ben Drew. 2012.

It Happened Here. Dir. Kevin Brownlow and Andrew Mollo. 1964.

Les Glaneurs et la glaneuse. Dir. Agnès Varda. 2000.

London Orbital. Dir. Chris Petit and Iain Sinclair. 2002.

London – The Modern Babylon. Dir. Julien Temple. 2012.

Lost Landscapes of Detroit. Dir. Rick Prelinger. 2010.

Oil City Confidential. Dir. Julien Temple. 2009.

Profit Motive and the Whispering Wind. Dir. John Gianvito. 2007.

Radio On. Dir. Chris Petit. 1979.
Requiem for Detroit? Dir. Julien Temple. 2010.
Swandown. Dir. Andrew Kötting. 2012.
The Battle of Orgreave. Dir. Mike Figgis. 2001.
The Filth and the Fury. Dir. Julien Temple. 2000.
The French Connection. Dir. William Friedkin. 1971.
The Long Good Friday. Dir. John Mackenzie. 1980.
The Road. Dir. John Hillcoat. 2009.
The Silent Village. Dir. Humphrey Jennings. 1943.
The Wild Places of Essex. Dir. Andrew Graham-Brown. 2009.

ACKNOWLEDGEMENTS

Among those who have heard or read versions of some of the material that has found its way into this book, or with whom I have had the opportunity to discuss, over the years, the topics explored here, I would like to thank in particular John Armitage, Luke Bennett, Ryan Bishop, Lucy Bond, Neil Campbell, Georgina Colby, Matthew Cornford, David Cunningham, Mark Dorrian, Stephen Graham, David Holloway, Simon Perril, Steve Rowell, John Timberlake, Nick Ward, Neal White, Anne Whitehead and Leigh Wilson. At Reaktion, I am grateful to Ben Hayes for getting me started, and to Michael Leaman for helping me finish. Some parts of Chapter Four were previously published, in earlier iterations, in *Cultural Politics* and in *The Routledge Companion to Military Research Methods*.

PHOTO ACKNOWLEDGEMENTS

The author and publishers wish to express their thanks to the below sources of illustrative material and/or permission to reproduce it:

Photo Hildegard Blom, reproduced courtesy Stroom Den Haag: p. 116; © Stan Douglas, courtesy the artist, Victoria Miro and David Zwirner: p. 97; Library of Congress, Prints and Photographs Division, Washington, DC: p. 94; reproduced by kind permission of Chris Petit and Iain Sinclair: p. 73; Photofusion/Shutterstock: p. 57; photo © Tate: p. 26; photo Corine Vermuelen, courtesy Mike Kelley Foundation for the Arts/© Estate of Mike Kelley – All Rights Reserved/VAGA at ARS, NY and DACS, London 2020: p. 112.

INDEX